THE
FIVE PILLARS
OF DISCIPLESHIP

CHIMA E. UMEJIAKU

WESTBOW
PRESS®
A DIVISION OF THOMAS NELSON
& ZONDERVAN

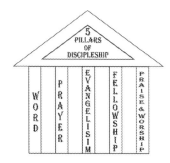

WestBow Press books may be ordered through booksellers or by contacting:

WestBow Press
A Division of Thomas Nelson & Zondervan
1663 Liberty Drive
Bloomington, IN 47403
www.westbowpress.com
1 (866) 928-1240

Because of the dynamic nature of the Internet, any web addresses or links contained in this book may have changed since publication and may no longer be valid. The views expressed in this work are solely those of the author and do not necessarily reflect the views of the publisher, and the publisher hereby disclaims any responsibility for them.

Any people depicted in stock imagery provided by Getty Images are models, and such images are being used for illustrative purposes only.
Certain stock imagery © Getty Images.

Interior Image Credit: JIL C. UMEJIAKU

Scripture taken from the King James Version of the Bible.

Scripture taken from the New King James Version®. Copyright © 1982 by Thomas Nelson. Used by permission. All rights reserved.

Scripture taken from the Amplified Bible, Copyright © 1954, 1958, 1962, 1964, 1965, 1987 by The Lockman Foundation. Used with permission.

Scripture taken from The Message. Copyright © 1993, 1994, 1995, 1996, 2000, 2001, 2002. Used by permission of NavPress Publishing Group.

ISBN: 978-1-9736-8704-7 (sc)
ISBN: 978-1-9736-8703-0 (hc)
ISBN: 978-1-9736-8705-4 (e)

Library of Congress Control Number: 2020904949

Print information available on the last page.

WestBow Press rev. date: 03/13/2020

I dedicate this book to Brother Augustine and Sister Rosa Lodato; Sister Anna Cavallo; Sister Patricia M. O'Sullivan; Brother Joe and Tina Freni; and Rev. Michael and Connie Player for their input into this project. I also thank Pastor Frank and Sister Maureen Fodera; Pastor Chuks and Sister Divine Ezewuzie; and Pastor John and Sister Helen Erevwiohwo for their love, encouragement, and support to my family and for the work of the Lord in the Christian Assembly Churches in Lynn and Lowell, Massachusetts.

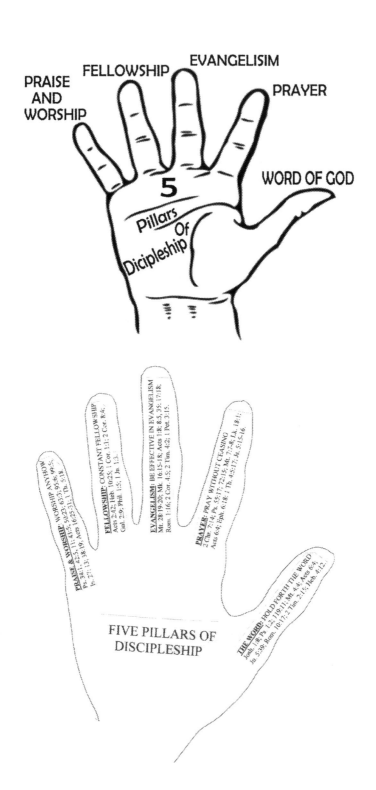

PRAISE AND WORSHIP

FELLOWSHIP

EVANGELISIM

PRAYER

WORD OF GOD

5 Pillars Of Dicipleship

PRAISE & WORSHIP: WORSHIP ANYHOW
Ps. 34:1, 42:5, 11; 43:5; 50:23; 63:3; 95:6, 99:5;
Is. 27: 13; 38:19; Acts 16:25-31; 1 Th. 5:18

FELLOWSHIP: CONSTANT FELLOWSHIP
Acts 2:42; Heb. 10:25; 1 Cor. 1:1; 2 Cor. 8:4;
Gal. 2:9; Phil. 1:5; 1 Jn. 1:3

EVANGELISIM: BE EFFECTIVE IN EVANGELISIM
Mt. 28:19-20; Mk. 16:15-18; Acts 1:8; 8:5, 35; 17:18;
Rom. 1:16; 2 Cor. 4:5; 2 Tim. 4:2; 1 Pet. 3:15.

PRAYER: PRAY WITHOUT CEASING
2 Chr. 7:14; Ps. 55:17; 72:15; Mt. 7:7-8; Lk. 18:1;
Acts 6:4; Eph. 6:18; 1 Th. 4:5:17; Js. 5:15,16.

THE WORD: HOLD FORTH THE WORD
Josh. 1:8; Ps. 1:2; 119:11; Mt. 4:4; Acts 6:4;
Jn. 5:39; Rom. 10:17; 2 Tim. 2:15; Heb. 4:12.

FIVE PILLARS OF DISCIPLESHIP

Contents

List of Illustrations

Foreword

Dr. Chima Umejiaku, a seasoned and experienced Christian for decades by the grace of God, has written this little book, *The Five Pillars of Discipleship,* which expresses very fundamental biblical truths that are rare to come by in our present day.

The unambiguous truth about discipleship, which the church of today has either downplayed or ignored, is the bane of church growth today. The only way to have a strong, vibrant, and living church is for disciples to multiply or propagate themselves. Many people in the church today are just there, seeking after "bread and fish" or some other miracle, yet living lives that are contrary to the Word of Christ, the Bible. Such individuals are not able to stand for Christ as his representatives or disciples, neither can they make disciples when they do not have a standing with Christ. This is because people cannot give what they do not have. It is, therefore, an imperative for a Christian to become a disciple. This is only possible by training and teaching Christians who have become subject to the yoke of Christ.

This little book emphasizes the need for this teaching, which will eventually establish the life of Christ in these new disciples and thus enable them to live and become effective witnesses of Jesus Christ in their community and wherever they go.

I therefore recommend this book to enable a wide readership and use of the material therein so that the body of Christ may benefit from this timeless truth.

Ishmael Ogboru, PhD
Professor of Economics and Chaplain, the Chapel of Faith, University of Jos, Nigeria

Preface

Christian discipleship is a biblical fundamental trust that was demonstrated in the ministry of Jesus Christ and also within the early church, as seen in the book of Acts. Knowing the importance of discipleship, Jesus walked closely with his disciples to influence their lives so they could, in turn, influence the world. He employed several kinds of teachings, modelings, demonstrations, and illustrations of familiar parables to drive home his messages.

The impact that Jesus's teachings had on the disciples was felt around the world for many generations, as the early disciples endeavored to fulfill the Great Commission mandate, as stated in Matthew 28:19–20, Mark 16:15–16, and Acts 1:8.

Emphasis on the importance of Christian discipleship is lacking today within Christendom, and this can be seen in the kind of believers we produce. It is obvious that we are seeing a generation that is not deeply rooted in the basic principles of Christianity. Proper Christian discipleship will not only equip believers; it also will establish in them the basic biblical truths they will pass on to the incoming generation.

The purpose of this book is to call on pastors and ministers of the gospel to go back to the fundamental truth of biblical discipleship to equip both old and new converts, so they can effectively carry on the work of ministry and thereby influence the world.

Acknowledgments

I want to thank the members of Christian Assembly Church in Lynn and Lowell, Massachusetts, for their support, encouragement, and request to publish all the teachings we've had during discipleship trainings. This would not have been possible were it not for your persistent calls and constant reminder that you wanted something to help new converts to our churches. I want to thank Sister Chioma Onyeukwu who, through due diligence, made necessary corrections from the beginning of this write-up until the finishing point. I also want to thank my wife, Pastor Favour Umejiaku, for her unalloyed support, and my son, JIL Umejiaku, who provided the illustrations used in this book. I am deeply grateful to Deborah Beatty Mel for her critical evaluation and contributions to this project. Lastly, I thank the almighty God for the grace and wisdom to put this material together so it would be a blessing to the body of Christ worldwide.

Introduction

As we discuss the five pillars of Christian discipleship, it is imperative that we consider these two phrases: "that you have eternal life" or "that you may know that you have eternal life." Being absolutely aware that you have eternal life in Jesus Christ was important to John the beloved; therefore, it was a common phrase in his writings. The phrase can be found in both the Gospel and Epistles of John. For example:

- "And this is eternal life, that they may know You, the only true God, and Jesus Christ whom You have sent" (John 17:3).
- "But these are written that you may believe that Jesus is the Christ, the Son of God, and that believing you may have life in His name" (John 20:31).
- "These things I have written to you who believe in the name of the Son of God, that you may know that you have eternal life, and that you may continue to believe in the name of the Son of God" (1 John 5:13).

Assurance of Salvation

We shall examine in this study the following questions: How do you know that you have eternal life? Will eternal life be realized here on earth or when we get to heaven? What does it mean to become born again? What does it mean to be a new creature in Christ?

"That You Have Eternal Life"

John, one of the apostles of Jesus Christ, wrote 1 John around AD 85–95, probably from Ephesus. He wrote this Epistle for three reasons. First, he wanted to combat the increasing threat of false teachers who were prevalent at that time. The false teachers denied that Jesus had come in the flesh (1 John 4:2–3). Second, he wrote to reassure believers of their faith and confidence in God, especially that they may be aware that they have eternal life (1 John 5:13). Third, he wanted them to know that believers have passed from death to life (1 John 3:14, 2:25; John 5:24, 20:31). This is important because Jesus Christ himself is the source of life (John 14:6).

The concept of knowing that we have eternal life is common in the Epistle of 1 John, and this absolute confidence is necessary for a firm foundation in Christian faith (1 John 1:12; 2:25; 4:9; 5:11, 13, 20). This assurance of eternal life in Christ opens a new relationship with God; as the apostle Paul puts it, we become heirs with Christ, and we can equally call God our Father:

- "And if children, then heirs—heirs of God and joint heirs with Christ, if indeed we suffer with Him—that we may also be glorified together" (Romans 8:17).
- "For you did not receive the spirit of bondage again to fear, but you received the Spirit of adoption by whom we cry out, Abba, Father" (Romans 8:15).
- "And because you are sons, God has sent forth the Spirit of His Son into your hearts, crying out, Abba, Father" (Galatians 4:6).

Our sonship in God through Christ provides unshakable assurance of our new position in him. We must know with certainty that we have eternal life: "These things I have written to you who believe in the name of the Son of God, that you may know that you have eternal life and that you may continue to believe in the name of the Son of God" (1 John 5:13).

How Can Believers Know with Absolute Certainty That They Have Eternal Life?

The apostle John answered this question in 1 John 5:12: "He who has the Son has life; he who does not have the Son of God does not have life." This eternal life, according to John, is the present possession of anyone who is in Christ. Believers ought to be convinced of their faith and trust in God with absolute certainty.

Eternal life is through the Son of God, Jesus Christ. Therefore, you must accept the lordship of Jesus Christ to experience eternal life and inherit God's promises. The Bible, which is the Word of God, stated that we can know with absolute certainty that we have eternal life (1 John 5:13). Those who are born again must have this assurance and confidence as they submit to God's authority through His Word (2 Timothy 3:16–17; 2 Peter 1:19–21). Believers must have the witness in themselves: "He who believes in the Son of God has the witness in himself; he who does not believe God has made Him a liar, because he has not believed the testimony that God has given of His Son. And this is the testimony that God has given us eternal life, and this life is in His Son" (1 John 5:10–11). The apostle Paul, in his own contribution, stated, "The Spirit Himself bears witness with our spirit that we are children of God" (Romans 8:16). You can be certain that you are a child of God through the witness of the Holy Spirit in you. In this case, you must reject every doubt and any contrary teaching, not relying on feeling but on an absolute faith and trust in God Almighty. The faith emanates from no other source but from the Word of God: "So then faith comes by hearing, and hearing by the word of God" (Romans 10:17).

Why Must We Know That We Have Eternal Life?

The reason to know that we have eternal life is the confidence to receive whatever we ask of the Father. "Now this is the confidence that we have in Him, that if we ask anything according to His will, He hears us" (1 John 5:14). This confidence that God answers prayer removes doubt, diminishes self-effort, and encourages total reliance on God. Sin separates from God and hinders prayer:

- "But your iniquities have separated you from your God; and your sins have hidden His face from you, so that He will not hear" (Isaiah 59:2).
- "For all have sinned and fall short of the glory of God" (Romans 3:23).
- "For the wages of sin is death, but the gift of God is eternal life in Christ Jesus our Lord" (Romans 6:23).

The redemptive death of Jesus Christ brought reconciliation to the Father as we put our faith in him through the Son. This trust in Christ makes us become new creatures and also acquire new positions in God's family.

> Therefore, if anyone is in Christ, he is a new creation; old things have passed away; behold, all things have become new. Now all things are of God, who has reconciled us to Himself through Jesus Christ, and has given us the ministry of reconciliation, that is, that God was in Christ reconciling the world to Himself, not imputing their trespasses to them, and has committed to us the word of reconciliation. Now then, we are ambassadors for Christ, as though God were pleading through us; we implore you on Christ's behalf, be reconciled to God. For He made Him who knew no sin to be sin for us, that we might become the righteousness of God in Him. (2 Corinthians 5:17–21)

Jesus's death on the cross was a predetermined plan of God: "Him, being delivered by the determined purpose and foreknowledge of God, you have taken by lawless hands, have crucified, and put to death" (Acts 2:23). That is to say, it was God's purpose that, through the death of his Son, the world would be reconciled to him (2 Corinthians 5:19).

The payment of sin was by the blood of Jesus Christ, because without the shedding of the blood, there is no remission of sin (Hebrews 9:22). In other words, God made Christ, who knew no sin, to become sin for humanity that the whole world might be reconciled to him (2 Corinthians 5:21). It was not the Jews who killed Jesus Christ; instead, Jesus died because of our sins.

Jesus Is the Only Way to God

Through his atoning death, Christ became the only way to reach God, contrary to many teachings today that we have other ways or means to God. "Jesus said to him, I am the way, the truth, and the life. No one comes to the Father, except through Me" (John 14:6). Similarly, the apostle Peter stated emphatically, "This is the stone which was rejected by you builders, which has become the chief cornerstone. Nor is there salvation in any other, for there is no other name under heaven given among men by which we must be saved" (Acts 4:11–12). This is what Isaiah 64:6 says: "But we are all like an unclean thing, and all our righteousness are like filthy rags; we all fade as leaf, and our iniquities, like the wind, have taken us away." No amount of self-righteousness or self-effort can make us earn salvation or heaven. It is only by grace through faith that we are saved (Ephesians 8:8–9). Remember that good work follows salvation, and not the other way around, for we are his workmanship, created for good works (Ephesians 2:10).

What Does It Mean to Be Born Again?

The concept of being born again proceeded from the lips of Jesus Christ to Nicodemus. "Jesus answered and said to him, 'Most assuredly, I say to you, unless one is born again, he cannot see the kingdom of God'" (John 3:3). The apostle Peter told us that we are born again through the incorruptible seed, which is the Word of God (1 Peter 1:23). Similarly, Paul said, "If you confess with your mouth the Lord Jesus and believe in your heart that God has raised Him from the dead, you will be saved. For with the heart one believes unto righteousness and with the mouth confession is made unto salvation" (Romans 10:9–10). Jesus is the free gift from God, and as you know, gifts are not earned but should be received freely. "But as many as received Him, to them He gave the right to become children of God, to those who believe in His name" (John 1:12).

You can pray the sinner's prayer below if you have never received Jesus Christ as your personal Savior and if you want to be obedient to the Word of God:

The Sinner's Prayer

Lord Jesus, I now know that you are the only way to God. Thank you for dying on the cross for my sins. I invite you into my life, and I accept you as my Lord and Savior. By accepting you in my life, I now know that I have eternal life. Thank you, Lord, for this new relationship with you. Give me the grace to follow you diligently and the power to overcome sin, Satan, and the world. Holy Spirit, be my counselor and my teacher and my guide, in Jesus's name, amen.

CHAPTER 1

The Five Pillars of Discipleship

Then Jesus said to those Jews who believed Him, "If you abide in My word, you are My *disciples* indeed."
—John 8:31 (emphasis added)

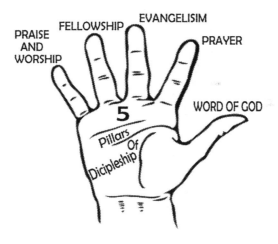

This diagram shows five basic areas of discipleship: always study God's Word, engage in daily prayer, be effective in evangelism, have constant fellowship with other believers, and live a life of constant worship and thankfulness to God. Each finger represents a step in spiritual growth. The thumb represents the Word of God, the index finger is prayer, the middle finger is evangelism, the ring finger is fellowship, and the smallest finger is for praise and worship. These are five basic principles of spiritual growth, which, if maintained, will always keep the believer on fire for God. Some of the materials in this book were taken from a 2017 book by the author.[1] We shall now discuss each one of them in detail, starting with the Word of God.

The Importance of Always Studying God's Word

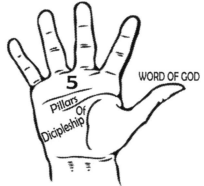

"**This Book of the Law** shall not depart from your mouth, but you shall meditate in it day and night, that you may observe to do according to all that is written in it. For then you will make your way prosperous, and then you will have good success." (Joshua 1:8, NKJV).

Guiding Principles for Studying the Scriptures

As you begin to study God's Word during quiet times (any convenient period you can set aside daily to meet with him), reflecting on the following questions will enhance your understanding and practical experience as a Bible-believing Christian:

- Is there any command or rule for me to keep or obey?
- Are there any characters for me to emulate from the passage?
- Are there some habits in my life to discontinue?
- Are there some sins in my life to confess before God?
- Are there any lessons from the passage for me to keep?

God's ultimate desire is to have a lasting relationship with all

---

[1] Chima E. Umejiaku, *Pursuit of Spiritual Renewal: A Call to Corporate and Individual Revival* (Maitland, FL: Xulon Press, 2017), 120–124.

believers—a relationship built on constant and renewable fellowship. This longing and desire for fellowship creates a bond, which is kept aflame by the fire of the Holy Spirit, flowing vertically from the throne of God and strengthening the horizontal relationship among the brethren. What does it mean to be aflame? The word *aflame* means to be on fire or blazing, and *blazing* means outstanding power, speed, heat, or intensity. In other words, a child of God ought to be zealous for the things of God. Here is the first principle: constant feeding on God's Word.

Let the Word of God Dwell in You Richly

Colossians 3:16 says, "Let the word of Christ dwell in you richly in all wisdom, teaching and admonishing one another in psalms and hymns and spiritual songs, singing with grace in your hearts to the Lord." When the Word of God dwells richly in you, then you will be able to encourage others through hymns, teaching others of God's Word, and singing spiritual songs that flow abundantly from your heart. On the contrary, you cannot offer anything meaningful from your heart when you are deficient of God's Word. Remember that you cannot give what you do not have.

Study God's Word Diligently

Second Timothy 2:15 instructs, "Study to show thyself approved unto God, a workman that needeth not to be ashamed, rightly dividing the word of truth" (KJV). A diligent study of God's Word will position believers to teach and influence other people by modeling Christ in their daily Christian living. Diligent study of God's Word ought to lead to right believing, and right believing will lead to right living.

Meditate on God's Word Day and Night

Joshua 1:8–9 says, "This book of the law shall not depart from your mouth, but you shall meditate in it day and night, that you may observe to do according to all that is written in it. For then you will make your way prosperous, and then you will have good success." (See also Psalm 1:1–2.) Take note of the phrase "then you will make your way prosperous, and then you will have good success." This seems to indicate that our spiritual prosperity is dependent on how much we know and meditate on the Word of God.

Search the Scriptures to Find Jesus and Eternal Life

John 5:39 says, "You search the Scriptures, for in them you think you have eternal life; and these are they which testify of Me." It is not bad to investigate about Jesus in theological, psychological, or philosophical books. However, apart from the Bible, other sources will give you a distorted view of who Christ is. You may even be led astray from your discoveries about him. Do you want to know more about Jesus, the only begotten Son of God? Search the scriptures, and you will be amazed about Jesus Christ of Nazareth and what the Bible said concerning him, both in the Old Testament prophecies and their fulfillment in the New Testament.

Always Desire Pure Milk

First Peter 2:2 states, "As newborn babes, desire the pure milk of the word, that you may grow thereby." Just as a newly born baby would desire pure milk from the mother's breast, the apostle Peter calls on all believers, whether new or old, to crave the unadulterated/undiluted Word of God, which is able to supply the required spiritual nutrients that cause the soul to be in constant tune with God. All believers should cultivate and develop a discerning spirit in order to ascertain what will kill or jeopardize their spiritual growth in Christ. Adulterated milk is very dangerous for any newborn, and as such, parents should be careful of what they feed their babies. Likewise, both new and old believers should be careful of the kind of spiritual food they consume.

God's Word Directs and Guides the Believer

Psalm 119:105 says, "Your word is a lamp to my feet and a light to my path." God's Word not only guides believers but also illuminates their path to prevent stumbling. According to John F. Walvoord and Roy B. Zuck,

> Old Testament prophecy is a light compared with the darkness of a squalid room. God's prophetic word is a light, "an oil-burning lamp" (Ps 119:105), shining in a dark place. Though the world is darkened by sin (Isa 9:2; Eph 6:12), God's word, pointing to the future, enlightens believers about his ways. But the day of Christ's return (Rom 13:12) is coming. In the daytime, lamps are no longer needed. And a lamp is nothing compared with the Morning Star "Light-Bringer," [an expression] used only in 2 Peter 1:19. So, the Old Testament prophecy looks ahead to the coming of Christ, the bright Morning Star. (Rev. 22:16)[2]

The Bible is the Word of God, and in it, God revealed his character and his purpose of salvation through his only begotten Son, Jesus Christ (John 3:16). It contains God's redemptive plan of salvation and reconciliation for humanity right from the Old Testament (Genesis 3:15; 2 Corinthians 5:17–21), and it presents some ethical values on how individuals relate to one another and ultimately to God himself. For a matter of salvation, every individual requires a personal response to the accomplished work of Jesus Christ on the cross of Calvary.

---

[2] John F. Walvoord and Roy B. Zuck, *The Bible Knowledge Commentary: An Exposition of the Scriptures by Dallas Seminary Faculty* (Colorado Springs: Chariot Victor Publishing, 1983), 868–69.

Questions to Respond To

1. What efforts would you make to enrich your life spiritually through the Word of God?
2. How many verses of scripture would you memorize in the next six months? What strategies would you put in place to make this a reality?
3. Discuss the importance of daily studying of God's Word in the life of a Christian.

The Importance of Prayer in the Life of a Believer

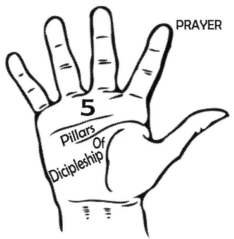

"**Praying** always with all prayer and supplication in the Spirit, being watchful to this end with all perseverance and supplication for all the saints" (Ephesians 6:18, NKJV).

We shall begin by describing the concept of prayer in the scriptures, according to Ronald F. Youngblood and his colleagues: "Prayer is communication with God. Because God is personal, all people can offer prayers."[3] However, the authors state, "Sinners who have not trusted Jesus Christ for their salvation remain alienated from God. So, while unbelievers may pray, they do not have the basis for a rewarding

---

[3] Ronald F. Youngblood, ed., *Nelson's New Illustrated Bible Dictionary,* rev. ed. (Nashville, TN: Thomas Nelson, 1995), 1022.

fellowship with God. They have not met the conditions laid down in the Bible for effectiveness in prayer."[4] The authors noted that prayer involves several important aspects, including faith, worship, confession, adoration, praise, thanksgiving, dedicated action, request, and effectiveness.[5] These are called the ACTS of prayer, an acronym for Adoration, Confession, Thanksgiving, and Supplication.

What Is Prayer?

Prayer is a means of communicating with God and making petitions to him regarding every need in our lives. We expect by faith that God will answer according to the promises in the scriptures and that he is ready to meet everyone at the point of their need.

Now we will briefly explore the concept of prayer in the scriptures based on the request of one of Jesus's disciples: "Now it came to pass, as He was praying in a certain place, when He ceased, that one of His disciples said to Him, Lord, teach us to pray, as John also taught his disciples" (Luke 11:1). "Lord, teach us to pray" was the heart desire of one of the disciples, and Jesus did not hesitate to show them a pattern of prayer. Responding to the request to teach his disciples how to pray, Jesus showed them a model of prayer, which was recorded in Matthew 6:9–13 and Luke 11:1–4. Here is Luke's version:

> So he said to them, when you pray, say, our father in heaven, hallowed be your name. Your kingdom come. Your will be done on earth as it is in heaven. Give us day by day our daily bread. And forgive us our sins, for we also forgive everyone who is indebted to us. And do not lead us into temptation but deliver us from the evil one. (Luke 11:1–4)

A careful look shows that Jesus gave this model of prayer (Matthew 6:9–13; Luke 11:1–4) on two separate occasions and under different

---

[4] Ibid.
[5] Ibid.

circumstances, and with some variations. Christ gave it in the Sermon on the Mount, while he was warning his disciples against ostentatious formality in prayer (Matthew 5:1, 6:5–13). He gave it again in an unnamed "certain place" in response to the request of a disciple, "Lord, teach us to pray" (Luke 11:1–4). It is obvious that this disciple had observed Jesus as he prayed numerous times (Luke 5:16, 6:12, 9:18, 11:1; Matthew 14:23; Mark 1:35) and then requested that Jesus should teach them how to pray. Although this is usually called the Lord's Prayer, obviously, it was not given to be recited each time we go to the Lord in prayer. Rather, it was given as an example of how we should model our prayer whenever we approach God with our petitions. There is no record in the New Testament that the disciples recited this prayer each time they prayed. This is evident in other prayers made by Jesus (John 17) and his disciples at different times in the New Testament, especially in the Synoptic Gospels or in the book of Acts (Acts 12).

The Prayer Life of Jesus

Jesus recognized the importance of prayer, so he lived a life of prayer to demonstrate and teach his disciples and all believers how to maintain constant communication and fellowship with the Father. Here are passages in the Synoptic Gospels that showed how Jesus prayed:

- He prayed and gave thanks to God while speaking with the Jewish leaders (Matthew 11:25–26).
- Before he walked on the water, Jesus went up on the mountain by himself to pray (Matthew 14:22–23).
- He gave thanks to God before feeding four thousand people (Matthew 15:36).
- He laid hands on little children and blessed them (Matthew 19:13–15).
- He prayed at the institution of the Lord's Supper (Matthew 26:26).
- He prayed three different times at the Garden of Gethsemane, where he surrendered his will to the Father (Matthew 26:36–46).

- He prayed while dying on the cross and said, "My God, My God, why have you forsaken me?" (Matthew 27:46).
- He went to a solitary place early in the morning and prayed (Mark 1:35).
- He prayed while healing a deaf and mute man (Mark 7:31–37).
- He prayed at his baptism (Luke 3:21–22).
- He withdrew into the wilderness to pray after healing certain people of their infirmities (Luke 5:15–16).
- He prayed all night before choosing his disciples (Luke 6:12–13).
- He prayed alone in a certain place before Peter confesses Jesus as the Christ (Luke 9:18–20).
- He prayed at the transfiguration (Luke 9:28–29).
- He prayed at the return of the seventy from evangelistic campaigns (Luke 10:21)
- He prayed before teaching his disciples how to pray (Luke 11:1).
- He prayed that Peter's faith would not fail him even as Satan wanted to sift him like wheat (Luke 22:31–32).
- He prayed immediately after he was nailed to the cross and asked the Father to forgive them, for they knew not what they were doing (Luke 23:34).
- While dying, Jesus prayed and committed his spirit into the Father's hand (Luke 23:46).
- After the resurrection, he blessed the bread before they ate (Luke 24:30).
- He prayed and blessed the disciples before his ascension into heaven (Luke 24:50–53).
- He prayed before feeding the five thousand (John 6:11).
- He prayed before raising Lazarus from the dead. (John 11:41–42).
- He prayed and asked the Father to glorify his name (John 12:27–28).
- His priestly prayer was for himself, his disciples, and all believers (John 17:1–26).

Indeed, Jesus left a legacy of prayer for believers of all ages.

Other Forms of Prayer in the Old and New Testaments

I want to make it clear that neither Jesus nor his disciples recited the model of prayer called the Lord's Prayer anywhere in the New Testament. I will now examine other forms of prayer in the New and Old Testaments so that we can see how people prayed in the past and received blessings from God.

First, let's examine the New Testament. Jesus prayed extensively during his earthly ministry, even though the writers of the Bible did not record everything he prayed about. At other times, he prayed simple prayers for sick ones; for instance, "For he said to him, 'Come out of the man, unclean spirit'" (Mark 5:8); "Lazarus, come forth" (John 11:43); and "Then he took the child by the hand, and said to her '*Talitha, cumi*,' which is translated, 'little girl, I say to you, arise'" (Mark 5:41). We can establish at this point that Jesus's priestly intercessory prayer, which is contained in John 17:1–26, is different from the pattern of prayer we saw in Luke 11:1–4, Matthew 6:9–13, or when he prayed for the sick and raised the dead, as we saw in the above passages.

In Acts 3:6, Peter prayed for a lame man: "Then Peter said, 'Silver and gold I do not have, but what I do have I give you: In the name of Jesus Christ of Nazareth, rise up and walk.'" Peter also prayed for Tabitha (Dorcas), who was dead: "But Peter put them all out and knelt down and prayed. And turning to the body he said, 'Tabitha, arise.' And she opened her eyes, and when she saw Peter she sat up" (Acts 9:40). Peter did not recite the Lord's Prayer in any of these incidents. He simply lifted up the lame man at the Beautiful Gate after he said, "In the name of Jesus of Nazareth, rise up and walk." On the other hand, he knelt down and prayed that the power of death should loosen its grip over Tabitha, and she immediately rose from the dead.

The disciples also prayed on many occasions. "Peter was therefore kept in prison, but constant prayer was offered to God for him by the Church" (Acts 12:5). Also, Paul and Silas prayed in prison: "But at midnight Paul and Silas were praying and singing hymns to God, and the prisoners were listening to them. Suddenly there was a great earthquake, so that the foundations of the prison were shaken; and immediately all the doors were opened, and every one's chains were loosed" (Acts 16:25–26). There was no record that Paul and Silas recited the Lord's Prayer in jail. Instead, it was recorded that they prayed and sang hymns, and God intervened in their situation by sending an earthquake that shook the foundations of the prison.

Paul prayed for the Ephesian church, offering prayers that the church might be rooted and grounded in the truth, because he understood the importance of a strong foundation.

> For this reason, I bow my knees to the Father of our Lord Jesus Christ, from whom the whole family in heaven and earth is named, that He would grant you, according to the riches of His glory, to be strengthened with might through His Spirit in the inner man, that Christ may dwell in your hearts through faith; that you, being rooted and grounded in love, may be able to comprehend with all the saints what is the width and length and depth and height, to know the love of Christ which passes knowledge; that you may be filled with all the fullness of God. (Ephesians 3:14–19)

Paul prayed for the believers at Ephesus purposely so they would comprehend all the fullness of God, to give them that sense of true spirituality and access to God's richest blessings and other resources made available in Christ.

Paul also prayed for the Colossian church. His prayer for them was related to fruitfulness, growth in the knowledge of God's will, and divine empowerment:

> For this reason, we also, since the day we heard it, do not cease to pray for you, and to ask that you may be filled with the knowledge of His will in all wisdom and spiritual understanding; that you may walk worthy of

the Lord, fully pleasing Him, being fruitful in every good work and increasing in the knowledge of God; strengthened with all might, according to His glorious power, for all patience and longsuffering with joy; giving thanks to the Father who has qualified us to be partakers of the inheritance of the saints in the light. He has delivered us from the power of darkness and conveyed us into the kingdom of the Son of His love in whom we have redemption through His blood, the forgiveness of sins. (Colossians 1:9–14)

Paul prayed that these brethren would understand God's deliverance from the tyranny of darkness and how they have been conveyed to the kingdom of light. His ultimate purpose was for them to realize their present status in Christ, because they had been made partakers of God's inheritance through Jesus Christ.

We shall now turn to other forms of prayer in the Old Testament. For instance, Abraham was a known intercessor. He pleaded for Sodom and Gomorrah, that God would spare the cities and not destroy them (Genesis 18:23–33). Solomon prayed at the dedication of the temple: "The Lord had said that He would dwell in a dark cloud; I have surely built you an exalted house, and a place for you to dwell in forever.... Then Solomon stood before the altar of the Lord in the presence of all the assembly of Israel, and spread out his hands ... and he said, Lord God of Israel, there is no God in heaven or on earth like You" (2 Chronicles 6:1–14).

Jehoshaphat prayed for God's intervention:

And Jehoshaphat feared, and set himself to seek the Lord, and proclaimed a fast throughout all Judah.... And Jehoshaphat stood in the assembly of Judah and Jerusalem, in the house of the Lord, before the new court, and said, O Lord God of our fathers, are You not God in heaven? And do You not rule over all the kingdoms of the nations ...?" (2 Chronicles 20:3–6).

King Jehoshaphat reminded God of his covenantal promise to Israel through Abraham, and God intervened and granted Judah victory over its enemies.

Nehemiah fasted and prayed to God: "So it was, when I heard these words, that I sat down and wept, and mourned for many days; I was fasting and praying before God of heaven. And I said: I pray, Lord God of heaven, O great and awesome God" (Nehemiah 1:4–11).

A careful examination of these prayers in both the Old and New Testaments shows that prayer did not take a particular pattern. Hence, we can conclude that the prayer commonly called the Lord's Prayer was a model that Jesus taught his disciples. Understanding the various patterns of prayer in the Bible will enable us to develop our own unique methods of communicating with God. In other words, we can offer the kind of prayer that touches God's heart by reminding him of his promises in the scripture.

We can approach God in prayer by adopting a conversational manner of petition, just like Abraham (Genesis 18:23–31), Hannah (1 Samuel 1:9–13), or Jesus (John 11:41–44). These kinds of prayer put the petition before God and believe that he will answer. The individuals we have examined so far reminded God of the promises he made to the Old Testament patriarchs such as Abraham, Isaac, and Jacob.

Another concept is praying the Bible. This is the idea of bringing the Word of God into conversational prayer with the Lord. It is based on reminding God about who he is, especially the progressive and multiple names in which he reveals himself as he meets the physical and spiritual needs of his children. These include *Jehovah-Jireh*, "the Lord will provide" (Genesis 22:13–14); *Jehovah-Rapha*, "the Lord who heals" (Exodus 15:26); *Jehovah-Nissi*, "the Lord my banner" (Exodus 17:8–15); *Jehovah-Shalom*, "the Lord our peace" (Judges 6:24); *Jehovah-Tsidkenu*, "the Lord our righteousness" (Jeremiah 23:6); and *Jehovah-Shammah*, "the Lord is present" (Ezekiel 48:35). The name of God is more than enough to supply every need his people might have. This kind of prayer that focuses on the progressive names of God also reminds us how faithful he has been in the past and tells of our unshakeable faith and confidence in him. As we critically examine the prayers of Jehoshaphat and Nehemiah, we discover that they reminded God of what he had done for Israel in the past; they also recalled his covenant with the patriarchs.

Why Should We Pray if God Already Knows Our Needs?

- We are commanded to pray in scripture (Matthew 7:7; Luke 18:1; 1 Thessalonians 5:17; 1 Timothy 1–2; Psalm 50:15; Jeremiah 33:3).
- We pray in order to maintain constant communication with God, because prayer offers us the opportunity to present our needs before him (Matthew 7:7; Hebrews 4:15–16).
- Prayer offers us the opportunity to confess our sins and receive forgiveness from God, thereby strengthening our relationship with him (Psalm 51:1–12; 1 John 1:8–9).
- Through prayer, we demonstrate our trust and obedience to God, as we acknowledge who is really in control of our individual lives.
- We are commanded to pray for the sick ones among us and believe God will heal them (James 5:13–15; Mark 16:15–18; Psalm 107:20; 1 Peter 2:24).

Prayer offers us the opportunity to present our petitions to God and trust him to intervene in difficult situations in our life. For example, Hannah was considered barren, but she prayed for a male child, and God answered her (1 Samuel 1:1–28). Peter was kept in chains, but the church prayed for him, and God sent an angel to release him from prison (Acts 12:1–19). Elijah prayed that God would withhold rain because of the sinful lifestyle in Israel, and God did so for three and a half years. He prayed again, and God brought rain in the land (James 5:17–18; 1 Kings 17:1).

We shall now turn to the next pillar: evangelism.

Questions to Respond To

1. Prayer is indispensable in the life of a Christian, just as water is indispensable in the life of a fish. Considering the facts in this statement, what would you do in order to maintain a healthy prayer life so as to live a victorious life?
2. Jesus maintained constant communication with his Father when he was here on earth. Therefore, he left for us a wonderful legacy of prayer in the Bible. Point out some practical examples of how he prayed in the Bible to substantiate this claim.
3. Why should Christians engage in prayer if they are aware that God already knows their needs? Give examples from the scriptures to support your answers.

The Importance of Evangelism by Every Believer

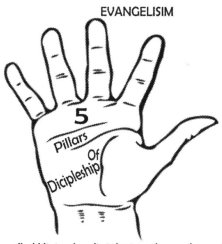

EVANGELISIM

"Then He called His twelve disciples together and gave them power and authority over all demons, and to cure diseases. He sent them to **preach the kingdom** of God and to heal the sick" (Luke 9:1-2, NKJV).

What Is Evangelism?

Evangelism is the proclamation of the kingdom of God in the fullness of its blessing and promise, which has also been called salvation. It involves

15

the proclamation and demonstration of God's reign and his kingdom on earth. The ministry of Jesus in signs and wonders was based on his relationship with the Holy Spirit, who is creative, imaginative, and inventive. The kingdom of God brings his reign into our lives when we make Jesus our Lord and Savior. The healing ministry of Jesus Christ demonstrated God's reign on earth and his power over sickness and demonic possession. In fact, evangelism involves a presentation of the good news of the Gospel, accompanied by the manifestation of God's presence and his power.

Jesus did more than preach the kingdom. He demonstrated its reality with signs of the kingdom, and there was public evidence that the kingdom he was talking about had come. We believe that signs should validate our evangelism efforts, because signs and wonders were not limited to the early apostles, as some people believe. Since the reason the Son of God appeared was to destroy the devil's work (1 John 3:8), he inevitably came into collision with the Prince of Darkness. The signs of the kingdom were evidence that the devil was retreating before the advance of the King. As Jesus put it, once the strong man has been overpowered by the stronger one, his possessions can be taken from him (Matthew 12:29; Luke 11:22). Jesus, the sinless Son of God, came to restore the authority man lost at the Fall (Genesis 3:15). Those who submit to God's grace through faith in Jesus will ultimately reign with him, because the kingdom authority has been restored through Jesus.

Who Should Be Involved in Evangelism?

"And Jesus came and spoke to them, saying, 'All authority has been given to Me in heaven and on earth. Go therefore and make disciples of all the nations, baptizing them in the name of the Father and of the Son and of the Holy Spirit, teaching them to observe all things that I have commanded you; and lo, I am with you always, even to the end of the age'" (Matthew 28:18–20). Jesus also said after his resurrection, "But you shall receive power when the Holy Spirit has come upon you; and you shall be witnesses to Me in Jerusalem, and in all Judea, and Samaria, and to the end of the earth" (Acts 1:8). This instruction to witness for Christ is given to every believer. Therefore, it is the responsibility of the church to mobilize its members to engage in evangelism. The church should announce and demonstrate the kingdom of God through the power of the Holy Spirit. Kingdom evangelism involves power evangelism, which transcends rational thinking. In other words, it involves evangelism that demonstrates God's power in signs and wonders; it introduces the reign of God in people's lives.

Six Biblical Methods of Evangelism

Listed below are six methods that can be utilized for effective personal evangelism. You don't have to use all the methods at the same time. It is advisable that you memorize one or two of them, but use one method at a time during your personal evangelism outreach. These six methods are the following: Solomon's words of wisdom for sinners, Isaiah's prophecy of redemption, journey through the Gospel of John, the apostle Paul's Roman map, Peter's salvation story, and Paul's message of reconciliation.

Solomon's words of wisdom for sinners: Solomon's advice is for sinners to forsake their evil ways and return to God Almighty.

- Consider the path you walk: "Ponder the path of your feet and let all your ways be established. Do not turn to the right or the left; remove your foot from evil" (Proverbs 4:26–27). Consider your ways, forsake the evil path, and walk in righteousness.
- Sinners wrong their own souls: "But he who sins against me wrongs his own soul; all those who hate me love death" (Proverbs 8:36). Sinners will face the consequences of their actions in this life or in the life to come, and they ought to be warned.
- Do not mock sin at any time: "Fools mock at sin, but among the upright there is favor" (Proverbs 14:9). It is dangerous to play with sin.
- Forsake the way that leads to death: "There is a way that seems right to a man, but its end is the way of death" (Proverbs 14:12).

It is advisable to forsake the evil way and walk the path that leads to eternal life.

- Confess your sin and receive pardon from God: "He who covers his sins will not prosper, but whoever confesses and forsakes them will have mercy" (Proverbs 28:13). Confessing our sins and receiving pardon from God is the acceptable way of repentance and receiving forgiveness.

Isaiah's Prophecy of Redemption: Following are passages in the book of Isaiah that talk about salvation, which every believer can utilize during soul-winning efforts:

- The great invitation: "Come now, and let us reason together, says the Lord, though your sins are like scarlet, they shall be as white as snow; though they be red like crimson, they shall be as wool. If you are willing and obedient, you shall eat the good of the land; but if you refuse and rebel, you shall be devoured by the sword; for the mouth of the Lord has spoken" (Isaiah 1:18–20). This is a great invitation from God Almighty, demanding absolute obedience that would usher in a life of blessing and fruitfulness, for anyone who answers the call.
- We have all wandered away from God: "All we like sheep have gone astray; we have turned, everyone, to his own way; and the Lord has laid on Him the iniquity of us all" (Isaiah 53:6).
- Our righteousness is like filthy rags: "But we are all like an unclean thing, and all our righteousness are like filthy rags; we all fade as a leaf, and our iniquities, like the wind, have taken us away. And there is no one who calls on Your name, who stirs himself up to take hold of You; for You have hidden Your face from us and have consumed us because of our iniquities" (Isaiah 64:6–7).
- Hell is open to swallow sinners: "Therefore Sheol has enlarged itself and opened its mouth beyond measure; their glory and their multitude and their pomp, and he who is jubilant, shall descend into it" (Isaiah 5:14). This passage was addressed to

those who call evil good and call good evil (Isaiah 5:20) and those who are wise in their own eyes (Isaiah 5:21). The rulers and people of Israel were attached to sin, which they dragged with them wherever they went, but they were not aware that all sinners will end up in hell. The question is: What kind of lifestyle are you living?

- Now is the time to seek God: "Seek the Lord while he may be found, call upon him while he is near. Let the wicked forsake his way, and the unrighteous man his thoughts; let him return to the Lord, and he will have mercy on him; and to our God, for he will abundantly pardon" (Isaiah 55:6–7).

You can ask people to commit their lives to Christ after hearing the Word of God from these passages. Isaiah 55:6–7 offers a unique opportunity for the sinner to return to God, who is willing to forgive every confessed sin.

Journey through the Gospel of John: The following are passages from the Gospel of John that present the salvation message:

- Jesus is a precious gift from God: "But as many as received Him, to them He gave the right to become children of God, to those who believe in His name" (John 1:12).
- The unconditional love of God: "For God so loved the world that He gave His only begotten Son, that whoever believes in Him should not perish but have everlasting life. For God did not send His Son into the world to condemn the world, but that the world through Him might be saved. He who believes in Him is not condemned; but he who does not believe is condemned already, because he has not believed in the name of the only begotten Son of God.... He who believes in the Son has everlasting life; and he who does not believe the Son shall not see life, but the wrath of God abides on him" (John 3:16–18, 36).

- Jesus is the light of the world: "Then Jesus spoke to them again, saying, I am the light of the world. He who follows Me shall not walk in darkness but have the light of life" (John 8:12).
- The truth shall set you free: "And you shall know the truth, and the truth shall make you free.… Therefore if the Son makes you free, you shall be free indeed" (John 8:32, 36).
- Jesus is the only way to God: "Jesus said to him, I am the way, the truth, and the life, No one comes to the Father except through me" (John 14:6).

At this point, you can give people a chance to respond to the Gospel by committing their lives to Christ. Do not get into an unnecessary argument about whether Jesus is the only way or not. Just present the Gospel, and allow the Holy Spirit to minister to the person. You can allow another believer who is more knowledgeable in the scriptures to answer any difficult questions or make some contributions.

The apostle Paul's Roman map.[6] Here are the apostle Paul's salvation messages, as contained in the book of Romans:

- We are all sinners before God: "For all have sinned and fall short of the glory of God" (Romans 3:23).
- Justification by faith brings the peace of God: "Therefore, having been justified by faith, we have peace with God through our Lord Jesus Christ" (Romans 5:1). The word *justification* means being declared righteous in God's sight; that is to say, we are as if we have never sinned before when we surrender our lives totally to Christ.
- God's love demonstrated toward sinners: "But God demonstrates His own love toward us, in that while we were still sinners, Christ died for us. Much more then, having now been justified by His blood, we shall be saved from wrath through Him. For if when we were enemies we were reconciled to God through

---

[6] Fellowship Tract League, Lebanon, Ohio.

the death of His Son, much more, having been reconciled, we shall be saved by His life" (Romans 5:8–10).

- The imputation of Adam's sin and Christ's righteousness: "For if by the one man's offense death reigned through the one, much more those who receive abundance of grace and of the gift of righteousness will reign in life through the One, Jesus Christ. Therefore, as through one man's offense judgment came to all men, resulting in condemnation, even so through one Man's righteous act the free gift came to all men, resulting in justification of life, for as by one man's disobedience many were made sinners, so also by one Man's obedience many will be made righteous" (Romans 5:17–19).

  The first Adam, being so naïve, went astray, and all people inherited his sinful nature, resulting in condemnation, but through the second Adam (Jesus Christ), justification was granted to all who will put their faith in Christ.

- The wages of sin is death, but Jesus offers eternal life: "For the wages of sin is death, but the gift of God is eternal life in Christ Jesus our Lord" (Romans 6:23). A sinful lifestyle has consequences, but on the other hand, God has the gift of eternal life for those who accept Christ as their Lord and personal Savior.
- Confession is with the mouth, and believing is in the heart: "That if you confess with your mouth the Lord Jesus and believe in your heart that God has raised Him from the dead, you will be saved. For with the heart one believes unto righteousness, and with the mouth confession is made unto salvation. For the Scripture says, whoever believes on Him will not be put to shame" (Romans 10:9–11).

  Confession with the mouth demonstrates and confirms the belief that is sealed in the heart.

Peter's salvation story. We have salvation messages from passages in Acts of the Apostles and the First Epistle of Peter.

- Jesus is both Lord and Christ: "Therefore, let all the house of Israel know assuredly that God has made this Jesus, whom you crucified, both Lord and Christ. Now when they heard this, they were cut to the heart, and said to Peter and the rest of the apostles, 'Men and brethren, what shall we do?' Then Peter said to them, 'Repent, and let every one of you be baptized in the name of Jesus Christ for the remission of sins; and you shall receive the gift of the Holy Spirit. For the promise is for you and to your children, and to all who are afar off, as many as the Lord our God will call'" (Acts 2:36–39).

  Peter called his audience to repentance after they heard the message of salvation. Confession, repentance from sin, and baptism seem to be mutually inclusive, as one comes to the knowledge of the truth.

- Christ's suffering and death was a fulfilled prophecy: "But those things which God foretold by the mouth of all His prophets, that the Christ would suffer, He has thus fulfilled. Repent therefore and be converted that your sins may be blotted out, so that times of refreshing may come from the presence of the Lord" (Acts 3:18–19).

  Repentance from sin ushers the presence of God into the life of the believer.

- Christ, the rejected stone, is the chief cornerstone: "This is the stone, which was rejected by you builders, which has become the chief cornerstone. Nor is there salvation in any other, for there is no other name under heaven given among men by which we must be saved" (Acts 4:11–12). Jesus is the only one, and there is no other one through whom people might be saved.

- God the Father raised Christ from the dead: "But Peter and the other apostles answered and said: We ought to obey God rather than men. The God of our fathers raised up Jesus whom you murdered by hanging on a tree. Him God has exalted to His right hand to be Prince and Savior, to give repentance to Israel and forgiveness of sins. And we are His witnesses to these things, and so also is the Holy Spirit whom God has given to those who obey Him" (Acts 5:29–32).

  God sent Jesus to die on the cross, and he also raised Christ from the dead to provide forgiveness of sins to those who will believe in His name.

- The blood of Jesus provides redemption: "You were not redeemed with corruptible things, like silver or gold, from your aimless conduct received by tradition from your father, but with the precious blood of Christ, as of a lamb without blemish and without spot" (1 Peter 1:18–19). Jesus's spotless blood provides redemption to all who acknowledge Him as their Lord and Savior. Sinners are redeemed (freed) by payment (Christ's blood) of a ransom price, just as slaves were redeemed in the ancient world.

Paul's message of reconciliation. These messages of reconciliation are found in the Pauline Epistles, such as 1 and 2 Corinthians, Galatians, Ephesians, and Colossians.

- A cross-centered message is foolishness to those who are perishing: "For the message of the cross is foolishness to those who are perishing, but to us who are being saved it is the power of God. For it is written: I will destroy the wisdom of the wise, and bring to nothing the understanding of the prudent.... For since, in the wisdom of God, the world through wisdom did not know God, it pleased God through the foolishness of the message preached to save those who believe" (1 Corinthians 1:18–19, 21).

- Repentant sinners are new creations in Christ: "Therefore, if anyone is in Christ, he is a new creation; old things have passed away; behold all things have become new. Now all things are of God, who has reconciled us to Himself through Jesus Christ, and has given us the ministry of reconciliation, that is, that God was in Christ reconciling the world to Himself, not imputing their trespasses to them, and has committed to us the word of reconciliation" (2 Corinthians 5:17–19).

Our identification with the risen Christ through faith not only makes possible the new creation but also now gives us responsibility for reconciling sinners to God, because we have received the ministry of reconciliation.

- Christ delivered us from this present evil age: "Grace to you and peace from God the Father and our Lord Jesus Christ, who gave Himself for our sins, that He might deliver us from this present evil age, according to the will of our God and Father" (Galatians1:3–4). Christ's mission on earth was to deliver humankind from the powers of darkness and to translate us into the kingdom of Jesus Christ (Colossians 1:13).
- Dead in sin but made alive in Christ: "And you He made alive, who were dead in trespasses and sins … that at that time you were without Christ, being aliens from the commonwealth of Israel and strangers from the covenants of promise, having no hope and without God in the world. But now in Christ Jesus you who once were far off have been brought near by the blood of Christ" (Ephesians 2:1, 12–13).

People are spiritually and morally dead until they come to the knowledge of the truth. The acceptance of Jesus as Lord and Savior transforms our moral essence as we begin to live a new life in Christ through the Holy Spirit.

• We have redemption through his blood: "He has delivered us from the power of darkness and conveyed us into the kingdom of the Son of His love, in whom we have redemption through His blood, the forgiveness of sins" (Colossians 1:13–14).

It is important to realize that personal evangelism is not complete until you offer the recipient the opportunity to make a commitment to Christ. Therefore, you can ask people if they are willing to surrender their lives to Christ. Then you can pray the sinner's prayer (repeat after me):

> Lord Jesus, come into my life. I recognize that I am a sinner, and I desperately need you. With my mouth, I confess that you died on the cross to save me. I believe with my heart that God raised you from the dead. Today, I surrender completely to you. Be my Lord and Savior, in Jesus's name, amen.

Questions to Respond To

1. What is your understanding of the term "Great Commission?" In your own view, should every Christian engage in evangelism? Support your answers from the Bible, and give tangible examples to substantiate your view on this issue.
2. Assuming it is now one year since you accepted Jesus as your Lord and Savior, how many souls have you brought into the kingdom through your personal evangelism effort?
3. What strategies would you put in place to fulfill the mandate of the Great Commission, as stated in Matthew 28:19–20, Mark 16:15, and Acts 1:8?

The Importance of Fellowship in the Body of Christ

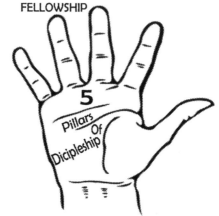

"And they continued steadfastly in the apostles' doctrine and **fellowship**, in the breaking of bread, and in prayers.(Acts 2:42, NKJV).

Then those who gladly received his word were baptized; and that day about three thousand souls were added to them. And they continued steadfastly in the apostles' doctrine and fellowship, in the breaking of bread, and prayer. Then fear came upon every soul, and many wonders and signs were done through the apostles. (Acts 2:41–43)

A proper understanding of the word *fellowship* will pave the way to grasp its importance and benefits within the body of Christ. From the above passage, we noticed four major things that preoccupied the early disciples after Pentecost: steadfastness in the apostles' doctrine, constant fellowship, breaking of bread (sharing), and constant prayer.

What is fellowship? According to Allen C. Myers, the word *fellowship* (*koinonia* in Greek) means "the communion or common faith, experiences, and expressions shared by the family of believers, as well as the intimate relationship they have with God."[7] Furthermore, the author states, "Although the concept is developed most fully in the New

---

[7] Allen C. Myers, *Eerdmans Bible Dictionary* (Grand Rapids, MI: Eerdmans, 1987), 380.

Testament, it is inherent in the Israel covenant. Grounded in the Lord's promise, 'I will be with you'" (Exodus 3:12, 16).[8] According to Ronald F. Youngblood and coauthors, the word *fellowship* means "sharing things in common with others. In the New Testament, fellowship has a distinctly spiritual meaning. Fellowship can be either positive or negative."[9] The authors, in order to shed more light upon the positive and negative sides of fellowship, further state that, positively, believers have fellowship with the Father, Son, and Holy Spirit (John 17:21–26). Those who have fellowship with Christ should enjoy fellowship with other believers, a communion that ought to illustrate the very nature of God himself (John 13:35; Ephesians 5:1–2; 1 John 1:5–10). Negatively, believers should not have fellowship with unbelievers. This means they should not share in unbelievers' sinful lifestyles (2 Corinthians 6:14–18). This does not mean, however, that believers should have no contact with unbelievers.[10]

The idea of Christian fellowship exists because of what Jesus accomplished for the body of Christ, that is, the church. This was fully demonstrated by the early disciples as they shared things in common, as stated in Acts 2:41–47, and the Lord manifested his power among them with signs and wonders. The relationship with God the Father, the Son, and the Holy Spirit is the basis for Christian fellowship, where people share mutual love, understanding, forgiveness, true oneness, and respect for each other. Fellowship is seen as an inner unity that, if nurtured properly, will eventually manifest outwardly in all aspects of believers' relationships. Within the Christian fellowship, believers are united in a common purpose; the same beliefs, aspirations, and goals; and their inclination to benefit one another by championing the cause of Christ in fulfilling the Great Commission mandate (Matthew 28:19–20; Acts 1:8).

It is important to point out that self-centeredness or selfishness can sometimes creep in unnoticed, but we can reinforce the true nature of Christian fellowship by constantly reminding ourselves of the goals of Christian faith. In other words, we must realize that our fellowship with

---

[8] Ibid.

[9] Youngblood, *Nelson's New Illustrated Bible Dictionary*, 449.

[10] Ibid., 449–50.

God takes precedence over all other relationships because, unless we are united with Christ in an established, undivided relationship, the inflow of the power of the Holy Spirit will not be available to strengthen the horizontal fellowship with others in the body of Christ. If you develop an intimate relationship with God, you will always long to have fellowship with members of the body of Christ. The psalmist said, "I was glad when they said to me, 'Let us go into the house of the Lord'" (Psalm 122:1). It should excite you whenever it is time to go to fellowship with other brethren.

Questions to Respond To

1. Some Christians these days are of the opinion that we can have fellowship through conference calls or join media churches as members; therefore, they have no need to attach themselves to any local church. What is your view on this matter?

2. The Bible commanded us to have fellowship with one another. Can you point out three verses from the scripture to support this claim?

3. Are there any benefits of belonging to a local church? Give specific examples from your local church or the early church, especially from the book of Acts.

The Importance of Christian Worship

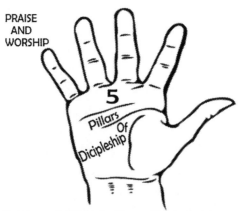

PRAISE AND WORSHIP

5 Pillars Of Dicipleship

"Let the word of Christ dwell in you richly in all wisdom, teaching and admonishing one another in **psalms and hymns and spiritual songs, singing with grace** in your hearts to the Lord." (Colossians 3:16, NKJV).

What Is Worship?

Worship is described as a reverential devotion to God in appreciation for his loving-kindness, protection, provision, or healing (Psalm 103:1–3). Worship was the method of approaching God in the Old and New Testaments. For example, in Genesis 22:5, "Abraham said to his young men, 'Stay here with the donkey; the lad and I will go yonder and *worship*, and we will come back to you'" (emphasis added). Abraham's worship of God was sacrificial in nature and demonstrated his commitment and obedience to God's instruction (Genesis 22:2). According to Allen Myers, "Worship (Heb. verb '*abad*', noun '*boda*'; Greek *proskyneo*) means to pay homage to or, literally, to ascribe worth to some person or thing. Hence, worship embraces the whole of the reverent life, including piety and liturgy."[11]

Looking at Christian history, we discover that worship has featured prominently as we endeavored to maintain a relationship with God, even though various methods were used in different settings. In describing certain elements of worship, James White quoted Martin Luther, who said that "in worship the people assemble to hear and discuss God's word and then praise God with song and prayer."[12] Thus, "worship has a duality, revelation and response, both of them empowered by the Holy Spirit."[13] We cannot rule out emotional involvement in worship, but the main thing is that it must come from the heart. Praise to God is not only an act of worship to him, but it is also a means of elevating worshippers into the presence of God, as they are lost in awe of God's majesty and glory. Those who offer praise glorify the Lord, and God will order their steps aright and show them his salvation (Psalm 50:23).

God alone should be our object in worship. Ronald Youngblood and his coauthors describe worship as "reverent devotion and allegiance pledged to God; the rituals or ceremonies by which this reverence is

---

[11] Myers, *Eerdmans Bible Dictionary,* 1067.

[12] James F. White, *Introduction to Christian Worship,* 3rd ed. (Nashville, TN: Abingdon, 2000), 22–23.

[13] Ibid., 23.

expressed."[14] They say the "English word 'worship' comes from the Old English word *worthship,* which denotes the worthiness of receiving the special honor or devotion."[15] Worship is an expression of God's love, mercy, and attribution of honor to him in celebration of the Eucharist, baptism, or special thanksgiving in acknowledgment of his majesty and faithfulness. According to James White, "The joy of Christian worship is reflected in singing; as you sing Psalms and hymns and spiritual songs among yourselves, singing and making melody to the Lord in your hearts" (Ephesians 5:19; Colossians 3:16).[16] White also noted that the celebration of the Eucharist remains the central form of worship for most Christians.[17] In fact, the Eucharist is celebrated throughout the Christian community. It is in this community that God is active in worship, as much as the worshipers themselves. As a response to God's work both in the past and in our midst, Christian worship is primarily and essentially an act of praise and adoration, which also implies a thankful acknowledgment of God's embracing love and redemptive loving-kindness.[18] Christian worship, irrespective of the denomination, features baptism, funeral rites, hymns, sermons or homilies, and the collection of an offering, all rooted in Bible tradition. "Now concerning the collection for the saints, as I have given orders to the churches of Galatia, so you must do also" (1 Corinthians 16:1).

What is true Christian worship? Those who wish to worship God must do it according to biblical instruction; God needs to be worshipped in spirit and truth (John 4:24), in reverential godly fear (Hebrews 12:28), not in vain or in hypocrisy (Matthew 15:9), and in an acceptable form of worship to him (Romans 12:1–2).

It is important to reference D. James Kennedy in what he called "five means of growth." Kennedy outlined the following as the means of spiritual growth in the context of Christian discipleship:

---

[14] Youngblood, *Nelson's New Illustrated Bible Dictionary,* 1321.

[15] Ibid.

[16] James F. White, *A Brief History of Christian Worship* (Nashville, TN: Abingdon, 1993), 36.

[17] Ibid., 55.

[18] Ibid., 23.

- **The Bible:** The reading in 1 Peter 2:2 stresses the importance of feeding on the Word of God.
- **Prayer:** This is a means of conversing with God in simple language from the heart, expressing love to him.
- **Worship:** Encourage new believers to engage in constant worship, and if they are already attending a Bible-teaching church, encourage them to continue to worship there faithfully.
- **Fellowship:** Stress to new believers the importance of fellowship, which could be termed "two or more fellows on the same ship." Every Christian needs to spend time with fellow believers for mutual encouragement, growth, and strength.
- **Witness:** Stress the importance of new believers confessing their faith to others through witnessing.[19]

What we see from Kennedy's contribution is similar to what is being promoted in this book, which is the Word, prayer, evangelism, fellowship, and praise/worship. Christians who practice these things will be spiritually strong and sound in Christian doctrine. All committed disciples of Christ should constantly evaluate their lives based on the concept of the five fingers. You cannot separate your prayer life from your Bible study life or from the three other components, as depicted in the above diagram. All are interrelated if you want to always grow in the grace of our Lord Jesus Christ (2 Peter 3:17–18).

Questions to Respond To

1. Discuss the importance of worship both in Old and New Testament times. How has worship influenced your life as a believer in Christ?
2. Worship comes in the context of fellowship and provides mutual encouragement, spiritual strength, and growth. What efforts

---

[19] D. James Kennedy, *Evangelism Explosion: Equipping Church for Friendship, Evangelism, Discipleship, and Healthy Growth,* 4th ed. (Carol Stream, IL: Tyndale, 1996), 106.

would you employ to see that you maintain quality time of praise worship in your personal life?

3. God inhabits the praise of his people (Psalm 22:3). Why do you think the devil doesn't want you to embark on praising God? What role did praise (worship) play in the lives of Old and New Testament believers? (Read 2 Chronicles 20 and Acts 16:25–31.)

The Assessment Day

It is recommended that you set aside one day each week to carry out an assessment of your spiritual life by asking these important questions: How was my Bible study life this week? Am I satisfied with my prayer life this past week? How many souls did I bring to Christ this past week? Am I always eager to be in the gathering of the saints? How is my present worship and praise life? Am I always honoring God whenever I worship? If you are honest to yourself, these questions will help you reflect on your spiritual condition and make amends where necessary.

We shall now investigate five Cs of Christian discipleship.

CHAPTER 2

Fundamentals of Christian Discipleship

But when He saw the multitudes, He was moved with compassion for them, because they were weary and scattered, like sheep having no shepherd.

—Matthew 9:36

The Five Cs of Christian Discipleship

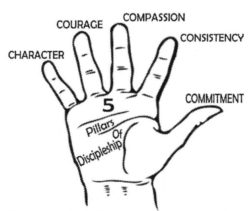

"Therefore, my beloved brethren, be steadfast, immovable, always abounding in the work of the Lord, knowing that your labor is not in vain in the Lord". (1 Corinthians 15:58 NKJV).

The five Cs of effective Christian discipleship are *commitment, consistency, compassion, courage,* and *character*. These qualities will produce and manifest tremendous virtues in the life of a child of God.

Commitment

This is defined as "an agreement or pledge to do something in the future, especially an agreement to assume a financial obligation on a future date; something pledged; the state or an instance of being obligated or emotionally impelled."[20] A commitment is a decision to carry out what we have pledged to do, no matter the cost. We are bound to hit roadblocks in life, but absolute commitment to champion the course of Christian duties will provide a boost to overcome any obstacles we might encounter along the way. Commitment is a good Christian virtue worthy of pursuing, because without it, our relationships with God and other believers will not be cordial. Commitment requires taking action or going through a certain path in life, even when it hurts.

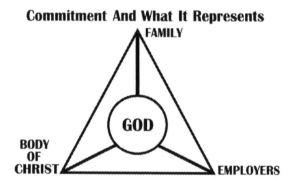

This diagram shows three things at the tips of the triangle: family, employers, and the body of Christ (the church). However, at the center is God. In order to live a fulfilled or balanced Christian life, you must allow God to influence your life so you can adequately carry out your obligations to family, employers, and the body of Christ. You must give equal attention to the three things to which you are obligated; otherwise, you cannot live a fulfilled Christian life. It requires an unalloyed commitment to follow Jesus Christ and pursue godly principles and a Christian character that would cause a believer to live a life that influences others within and outside the body of Christ.

---

[20] *Merriam-Webster's Collegiate Dictionary*, s.v. "commitment."

Jesus demanded commitment from his disciples when he made this statement: "Then He said to them all, 'If anyone desires to come after Me, let him deny himself, and take up his cross daily, and follow Me'" (Luke 9:23). Jesus invested so much in his disciples within the space of time they were together, and thus he would not expect anything less in return. It is not an overstatement to say that we lack Christian commitment in the body of Christ today, and this is adversely affecting the work of God.

Those who are unwilling to make a meaningful commitment to their marriages, careers, studies, or faith will not advance in life. Christian commitment requires sacrifices of time, money, and energy, with the conviction and assurance that God is faithful to his promises (Hebrews 10:23). A true disciple of Jesus Christ must be committed to the course of extending the kingdom by promoting all activities that gear toward soul winning, love of the brethren, and unity in the body of Christ. Everyone is committed to something. But there is one commitment that should supersede all other obligations, and that is commitment to God. In other words, God must be at the center of your commitment to be able to harness all other commitments in your life.

God must be at the center of your life to balance all daily activities as a Christian, but you need to give him the opportunity. You must meet certain obligations in order to be considered a committed member of a club or organization. For instance, let's assume that you belong to the Promise Keepers Club, where members are required to attend all meetings and contribute their monthly dues promptly. Anyone who fails to fulfill these two requirements would not be considered a committed member and, therefore, would not receive the benefits of the organization. Likewise, churches have obligations to be fulfilled by members. So it is required that believers should be committed to their families, employers, and the body of Christ. Christians who are committed to God are also committed to their families, employers, and the body of Christ. Some believers claim they are committed to God but do not attend prayer meetings or Bible study all year; it would be reasonable to have reservations about their commitment to God. Prayer meeting and Bible study are the most basic obligations expected of all believers in any congregation, but if the most important obligations are not carried out, what else will be carried out? The apostle Peter said, "But we must give ourselves continually to prayer and ministering of the word" (Acts 6:4). So prayer and the Word of God are two essential components of Christian commitment.

Consistency

What is consistency, and why is it necessary in Christian faith? *Consistency* is defined as the "condition of adhering together; firmness of material substances; ability to be asserted together without contradiction; harmony of conduct or practice with profession."[21] Synonyms of consistency include *constancy, stability, steadiness,* and *uniformity.* Consistency is how we display our conduct in a way that reflects stability or steadiness in our approach to matters of life. It is that aspect of our character that reveals our thoughts, desires, and practices and how we can harmonize issues. Consistency comes into play when our actions demonstrate our belief system and how we handle responsibilities assigned to us. A true disciple of Christ must endeavor to be consistent in character to be able to present fundamental principles of faith and engage in winning souls for the kingdom.

The apostle Paul admonished Titus to demonstrate a Christian character that reflected consistency in faith, as he was left on the island of Crete to put things in order: "In all things showing yourself to be a pattern of good works; in doctrine showing integrity, reverence, incorruptibility, sound speech that cannot be condemned, that one who is an opponent may be ashamed, having nothing evil to say of you" (Titus 2:7–8). As a true disciple, you also should endeavor to be on fire for the Lord and not display the attitude of the Laodicean Christians, whom Jesus rebuked: "I know your works, that you are neither cold nor hot. I could wish you were cold or hot. So then, because you are lukewarm, and neither cold nor hot, I will vomit you out of My mouth" (Revelation 3:15–16). Do not be a lukewarm disciple.

---

[21] Ibid., s.v. "consistency."

Compassion

Compassion is defined as "sympathetic consciousness of others' distress together with a desire to alleviate it."[22] Synonyms of *compassion* include, among others, *mercy, kindness, pity, solicitude, tenderness, concern, charity*, and *care*. The New International Version Bible often calls God "compassionate" (Exodus 33:19; Deuteronomy 30:1–4; Nehemiah 9:16–18; Psalm 51:1, 86:15, 103:13, 116:5, 119:77, 145:8–9; Isaiah 30:18, 33:19, 49:10, 49:13, 54:10, 63:7; James 5:11). We have several passages in the scripture about the compassionate Savior: "But when He saw the multitudes, He was moved with compassion for them, because they were weary and scattered, like sheep having no shepherd" (Matthew 9:36). Jesus was moved with great compassion toward a great multitude and healed them (Matthew 14:14). He said to his disciples, "I have compassion on the multitude" (Matthew 15:32). Jesus also had compassion on a blind man; he touched him, and his sight was restored (Matthew 20:34). We can say without reservation that Jesus demonstrated incredible compassion as he ministered to the people during his earthly ministry. We are enjoined to have compassion toward one another (Psalm 112:3–5; Zechariah 7:9–10; Colossians 3:12; Ephesians 4:32; 1 Peter 3:8; Philippians 2:1–2). Therefore, as disciples of Jesus Christ, we cannot minister effectively until we have compassion for the people, whether within the body of Christ or among nonbelievers. Jesus's tender heart was the secret behind the success of his ministry, and as children of God, we must demonstrate tenderness toward the lost. We need to love them but hate the lifestyle they adopt. We cannot have a successful ministry until we develop the spirit of compassion, and this will come when we surrender totally to the leading of the Holy Spirit.

Courage

What is courage? According to Ronald F. Youngblood and his coauthors, courage is defined as "the strength of purpose that enables

---

[22] Ibid., s.v. "compassion."

one to withstand fear or difficulty. Furthermore, that physical courage is based on moral courage, a reliance on the presence and power of God and a commitment to His commandments (Josh. 1:6–7, 9, 18; 23:6; 2 Chr. 19:11)."[23] *Merriam-Webster's Collegiate Dictionary* defines courage as:

> mental or moral strength to venture, persevere, and withstand danger, fear, or difficulty. Synonyms of courage are mettle, spirit, resolution or tenacity. It means mental or moral strength to resist opposition, danger, or hardship. Courage implies firmness of mind and will, in the face of danger or extreme difficulty.[24]

It is not an easy thing to be a disciple of Jesus Christ; therefore, courage is a prerequisite if you want to stand firm to the end. Jesus emphatically said we would face opposition: "These things I have spoken to you, that in Me you may have peace. In the world you will have tribulation; but be of good cheer, I have overcome the world" (John 16:33). Paul told Timothy to endure hardship: "You therefore must endure hardship as a good soldier of Jesus Christ" (2 Timothy 2:3).

Character

Character is "one of the attributes or features that make up and distinguish an individual."[25] Development of godly character is paramount in the life of a disciple of Christ. What is character? According Dr. Richard J. Krejcir, "Character is defined as a collection of personality traits within our behavior that shows who we are. This is shown in our integrity, attitude, moral fiber, disposition, and this shapes how we treat one another, good or bad. This is mostly true, but it goes

---

[23] Youngblood, *Bible Dictionary*, 305.

[24] *Merriam-Webster's Collegiate Dictionary*, s.v., "courage."

[25] Ibid., s.v. "character."

much deeper than that. Character is who we are and it can be learned and built when we are in Christ."[26]

As seen already, disciples are apprentices or learners who want to be like their master, and this entails developing certain character traits. The development of Christian character by disciples is progressive in nature, and this is called *sanctification.* By this, the Holy Spirit molds and shapes disciples of Christ to conform to his image. The inner character that is developed makes disciples become Christlike, and it gradually begins to manifest in temperament, attitude, or lifestyle, as disciples acquire the mind of Christ (Philippians 2:5–7). Subsequently, they begin to manifest the fruit of the Holy Spirit, such as love, joy, peace, long-suffering, kindness, goodness, faithfulness, gentleness, and self-control. Circumstances of life will test them, but they will demonstrate a Christlike attitude, even in the worst situations. The disciples are expected to exemplify faithfulness during frailty; demonstrate kindness and goodness to the lost; and show self-control in times of hostility, patience during times of unnecessary delays, peace in the face of conflict, and love toward the unlovable. Disciples of Christ develop certain competencies such as praying, studying, and practicing the Word; building relationships through Christian fellowship; showing hospitality toward one another; and engaging in personal evangelism. These methods were adopted by the early disciples (Acts 2:42–44), and they eventually turned the world upside down (Acts 17:6).

True disciples of Christ must avoid any attitude or unwanted character that would repel others from Jesus. Christian character is built by exhibiting holiness, setting boundaries, modeling our lives to be Christlike, living honorably in the face of opposition, and avoiding enticement from the Evil One through ungodly associations. Development of Christian character comes through total submission to the Lord, and the by-product of that will be unalloyed commitment, unquestioned conformity to the will and purpose of God, absolute obedience, and total dependence on the leading of the Holy Spirit.

---

[26] Discipleship Tools: ["What Is Character?] Accessed July 25, 2029. https:// www. discipleshiptools.org.

Disciples must place Christian character ahead of any personal ambition, as this will determine how they have internalized what they learned.

Integrity is paramount when we talk of Christian character (Exodus 8:28–32; 1 Thessalonians 2:10–12). Godly character calls for a total commitment to Christ that demonstrates integrity, honesty, and faithfulness. It also goes with self-discipline that flows from self-control, a fruit of the Holy Spirit. Christian character is a true treasure to be pursued and acquired in order to be like Christ. It is related to acquiring an attitude of submission and acceptance of servanthood as we minister to one another in the body of Christ. Lastly, moral character is everything in Christian discipleship, because there must be a big difference from the old way of life (2 Corinthians 5:17).

Five Qualities of People of Destiny

Committed disciples of Jesus Christ ought to maintain certain moral qualities that distinguish them from the world. This quality of Christian discipleship is represented by the acronym PADDI, which stands for Probity, Accountability, Discipline, Dedication, and Integrity. These Christian qualities must be part of the five pillars of discipleship to be inculcated in all followers of Jesus.

Let a man so consider us, as servants of Christ
and stewards of the mysteries of God.
—1 Corinthians 4:1

Probity

Probity is "adherence to the highest principles and ideals, or uprightness."[27] Probity is the quality of having strong moral principles, honesty, and decency. There has been a significant shift away from the Bible's established moral standards to practices and norms that are foreign to Christian beliefs. We are living in a time when people prefer to adopt moral standards of their choice that deviate significantly from what is godly; at the same time, they want to impose these standards on others, even though such people might be in the minority. A typical example is the gay movement and gay rights. Irrespective of what society might accept as the norm, we as Christ's disciples must adhere to the highest moral principles that speak eloquently of what we believe and practice, and that is probity.

Accountability

Accountability is defined as "the quality or state of being accountable, especially an obligation or willingness to accept responsibility or to account for one's action."[28] It is a condition of being accountable to a responsibility given or one that is accepted willingly. The word *accountability* is related to liability, responsibility, and answerability. The disciples of the Lord Jesus Christ are answerable to him for their actions, and the apostle Paul had this in mind when he said, "Let a man so consider us, as servants of Christ and stewards of the mysteries of God. Moreover, it is required in stewards that a man be found faithful" (1 Corinthians 4:1–2). In two other passages, Paul emphatically said that we must give account to God (Romans 3:19, 14:12; 2 Corinthians 5:10).

Discipline

Discipline is defined as "training that corrects, molds, or perfects the mental faculties or moral character; a control gained by enforcing

---

[27] *Merriam-Webster's Collegiate Dictionary*, s.v. "probity."

[28] Ibid., s.v. "accountability."

obedience or order; orderly or prescribed conduct or pattern of behavior; self-control."[29] It is regarded as the practice of training individuals to comply with law and order. Individuals can discipline themselves in order to attain to certain goals in life. Therefore, disciples of Jesus Christ must apply discipline to every aspect of their lives, especially if they want to spend eternity with Christ in heaven. The apostle Paul said, "But I discipline my body and bring it into subjection, lest, when I have preached to others, I myself should be disqualified" (1 Corinthians 9:27). Self-discipline is necessary as we relate with others in the community of faith.

Dedication

Dedication is defined as a devotion or setting aside for a particular purpose or self-sacrificing devotion. It is the quality of being dedicated or committed to a task or purpose.[30] Paul and Silas faced false imprisonment at Philippi (Acts 16:16–34). Instead of complaining or murmuring, they praised God behind the prison bars, and the Lord sent an earthquake that shook the foundation of the prison, such that all the prisoners were supernaturally released from their chains. Paul was dedicated to the course of the gospel of Jesus Christ, and God not only prospered his ministry but also honored him before the people.

Integrity

Integrity is defined as "firm adherence to code of moral or artistic value; incorruptibility; an unimpaired condition; soundness; the quality or state of being complete or undivided: completeness."[31] Integrity means honesty; uprightness, probity, rectitude, honor.[32] Integrity means possessing the quality of being honest and acquiring strong moral principles and moral uprightness. It is a personality trait that

---

[29] Ibid., s.v. "discipline."
[30] Ibid., s.v. "dedication."
[31] Ibid., s.v. "integrity."
[32] Ibid.

makes people admirable and that must be cultivated by disciples of Christ. Integrity is a fundamental value in any existing relationship, and it is equated with sound moral and ethical principles. According to David Jeremiah, *integrity* comes from the word *integer*, which is a whole number in mathematics. Integrity is a mind-set and willingness to be and do what is wholly and completely right as defined by God, regardless of personal cost or place. Whether in public or private, there is congruence.[33]

Integrity implies wholeness or completeness; in other words, undivided or not variable, depending on circumstances. It also implies consistency of character, regardless of the situation of life. Disciples of Christ who pursue a life of integrity do not live according to varying circumstances. Integrity is not just a Christian virtue but also a critical element of a Christ-centered life. The basic tenets of integrity are honesty, trustworthiness, truthfulness, and dependability. People of integrity behave honorably when nobody is watching, especially when discharging their responsibilities. As a disciple of Christ, integrity ought to be your core value as you perform your job within and outside the body of Christ. Suffice it to say that certain nonbelievers would not like to live a life of integrity, but they would expect those who call themselves followers of Christ to demonstrate it.

What does the Bible say about integrity? Let's look at Proverbs 10:9: "He who walks with integrity walks securely, but he who perverts his ways will become known." Christ's disciples who walk with integrity will have a good reputation before God and other people, but those who neglect godly principles will be exposed. Proverbs 11:3 states, "The integrity of the upright will guide them, but the perversity of the unfaithful will destroy them." Disciples who pursue the path of integrity will be guided by God's wisdom, but those who follow corruption or falsehood will be destroyed. Proverbs 20:7 says, "The righteous man walks in his integrity; his children are blessed after him." This implies that men and women of integrity will leave a lasting Christian legacy for their children. David made a request from the Lord: "Let integrity

---

[33] David Jeremiah, *The Jeremiah Study Bible* (Nashville, TN: Worthy, 2013), 818.

and uprightness preserve me, for I wait for you" (Psalm 25:21). Let this be the desire of our hearts and everyday prayer, as we pursue godly principles.

The Principles of Christian Discipleship

Five Fundamental Principles Of Christian Service

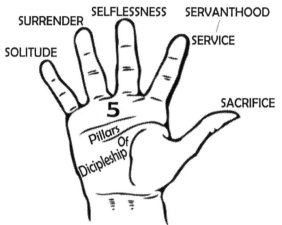

"As each one has received a gift, minister it to one another, as good stewards of the manifold grace of God". (1 Peter 4:10 NKJV)

This figure shows five fundamental principles of Christian discipleship: sacrifice, servanthood, selflessness, surrender, and solitude.

Sacrifice

Sacrifice is "an act of offering to a deity something precious, especially the killing of a victim on an altar; destruction or surrender of something for the sake of something else."[34] Sacrifice within the context of Christian discipleship is the willingness to make a tangible commitment toward the furtherance of the gospel of Christ. It could entail money, time, energy, or use of one's personal giftedness to serve members of the body of Christ. True disciples of Christ ought to discover their area of giftedness, develop it, and then use it for the benefit of other

---

[34] *Merriam-Webster's Collegiate Dictionary*, s.v. "sacrifice."

members of the Christian community. The apostle Peter puts it this way: "As each one has received a gift, minister it to one another, as good stewards of the manifold grace of God" (1 Peter 4:10).

There are certain Christians who understand what it means to make a sacrifice for other people. For instance, when I was in seminary, we had a brother in our Christian fellowship who would go out of his way to do extraordinary things for fellow seminarians. The brother was willing to sacrifice his time and would give away the last ten dollars he had in his pocket to anyone in need. Sometimes, he gave away his clothes without requesting anything in return. That attitude was so challenging that we could have called him "Brother Sacrifice." And that was exactly what happened during the early church when Brother Joses's name was changed to Barnabas, which means "Son of Encouragement" (Acts 4:36–37). The name was a result of his valuable contributions toward the growth of the newly formed church. God is still looking for believers who are willing to make tangible sacrifices toward building up the body of Christ.

Servanthood/Service

Our Lord Jesus Christ is our ultimate example when we talk of servanthood, and this is what he said: "For even the Son of Man did not come to be served, but to serve, and to give His life a ransom for many" (Mark 10:45). Jesus demonstrated the true nature of servanthood and service as he taught his disciples the act of humility.

> Jesus, knowing that the Father had given all things into His hands, and that He had come from God and was going to God, rose from supper and laid aside His garments, took a towel and girded Himself. After that, He poured water into a basin and began to wash the disciples' feet, and to wipe them with the towel with which He was girded. (John 13:3–5)

Servanthood goes with humility, and in God's economy, there is a reward associated with it. All these qualities are interwoven in the life of Jesus Christ. The apostle Paul dived into it as he explained the true nature of the humility and servanthood of Christ in Philippians 2:5–11. Jesus humbled himself and became obedient to the extent that he died a shameful death on the cross, but God in turn exalted him and gave him a name that is above all names. In fact, those who desire to attend greatness in God's kingdom must first be willing to serve others (Matthew 20:26).

Selflessness

The concept of selflessness is embedded in the ability to think of others better than ourselves. This is how the apostle Paul put it: "Let nothing be done through selfish ambition or conceit, but in lowliness of mind let each esteem others better than himself. Let each of you look out not only for his own interest, but also for the interest of others" (Philippians 2:3–4).

Focusing on the needs of others does not mean that we should ignore ourselves in the process; rather, we derive joy as we see the impact of our efforts in people's lives. Is it possible that we can meet all people's needs? Of course not. Any attempt to do that can lead to frustration and burnout. However, we must aim at serving others selflessly, with no strings attached, and leave the ultimate reward in God's hand, "for God is not unjust to forget your work and labor of love which you have shown toward His name, in that you have ministered to the saints, and do minister" (Hebrews 6:10).

Surrender

We must yield absolutely to the Holy Spirit in order to hear God's voice and carry out whatever instructions he might give. In other words, completely surrendering our lives to God will open many avenues as we walk with the Lord on a daily basis. The fruit of absolute surrender is the peace and tranquility that emanate from God, which is beyond human comprehension. "You will keep him in perfect peace, whose mind is stayed on You, because he trusts in You" (Isaiah 26:3). Absolute surrender to the Holy Spirit will not only bring God's peace in every circumstance of life; it will also dethrone our sense of self and keep it in check whenever it wants to raise its ugly head. The benefit of total surrender to the Holy Spirit is an obedient lifestyle that brings glory to the almighty God. On the contrary, we will experience a spiritual crisis in our walk with God when we do not practice the discipline of surrendering to the Lord.

Solitude

The discipline of Christian solitude is necessary in our daily walk with God. Jesus, who was the Son of God himself, practiced solitude when he walked on the earth: "Now in the morning, having risen a long while before daylight, He went out and departed to a solitary place, and there He prayed" (Mark 1:35). Jesus went to the mountainside and prayed all night (Luke 6:12); he prayed on the mountain (Matthew 14:23); he prayed at the Garden of Gethsemane (Matthew 26:36–56). In fact, Jesus maintained constant relationship with the Father throughout his earthly journey by his life of solitude. The life of solitude is necessary for all disciples of Jesus Christ, because it will offer us rest, rejuvenation, refreshment, restoration, and revival. This can be seen in the diagram.

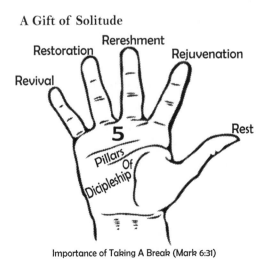

A Gift of Solitude

Importance of Taking A Break (Mark 6:31)

Solitude is also a time to refocus and strategize in order to be more effective in ministry. During Jesus's earthly ministry, he encouraged his disciples to rest. "And He said to them, 'come aside by yourselves to a deserted place and rest a while.' For there were many coming and going, and they did not even have time to eat" (Mark 6:31). Take note of the phrase, "And they did not even have time to eat." You can agree with me that not having enough time to eat when we are engaged in ministerial work can lead to both physical and spiritual burnout/exhaustion. Therefore, we need to learn to take a break to refresh and become more active in ministry.

It is therefore necessary for disciples of Christ to inculcate these fundamental Christian principles of sacrifice, servanthood, selflessness, surrender, and solitude. The impact of these principles will revolutionize our ministry as we serve one another within the Christian community.

Answering the Call of God

Just as Jesus called his disciples one by one and commissioned them to reach the world with the gospel, so he called every believer for a specific task within the body of Christ. However, we shall discuss below the general calling for every believer.

A Call to Salvation

This is the initial calling or the point of entry to a new relationship with Christ. The Holy Spirit inducts us into the body of Christ (2 Corinthians 12:13) as we respond to the great invitation and learn the way of Christ, as written in Matthew 11:18–30: "Come to Me, all you who labor and are heavy laden, and I will give you rest. Take My yoke upon you, and learn from Me, for I am gentle and lowly in heart, and you will find rest for your souls. For My yoke is easy and My burden is light."

There is a great exchange that takes place as you answer this call: the yoke of Satan is broken as you take the yoke of Christ. The implication of taking Jesus's yoke upon yourself is to hook together with him for the rest of your life. You cannot do anything without his approval. For you to do otherwise means acting contrary to his will and deviating from his purpose for your life.

A Call to Abide in Christ

We see in John 15:1–16 the importance of abiding in Christ for fruitful living. What does it mean to abide in Christ? It means a life of fruitfulness and growing in him. It means witnessing and bearing fruit by bringing new converts into the kingdom. It means displaying godly virtues and Christian character worthy of emulation. It also means growing and knowing God more intimately as you draw your spiritual nutrients from him, just as a tree branch draws minerals from the roots. Jesus's call to a believer is to be valued above any other relationship. This is what we saw in Luke 9:57–62, which focuses on the cost of discipleship. The passage stated thus:

> Now it happened as they journeyed on the road, that someone said to Him, 'Lord, I will follow You wherever You go.' And Jesus said to him, 'Foxes have holes and birds of the air have nests, but the Son of Man has nowhere to lay His head.' Then He said to another, 'Follow Me,' But he said, 'Lord, let me first go and bury my father.' Jesus said to him, 'Let the dead bury their own dead, but you go and preach the kingdom of God.' And another also said, 'Lord, I will follow You, but let me first go and bid them farewell who are at my house.' But Jesus said to him, 'No one, having put his hand to the plow, and looking back, is fit for the kingdom of God.

Every individual Jesus encountered in the above passage had one excuse or another to give, but Jesus wanted them to be involved in what matters most, the preaching of the kingdom of God.

A Call to Witness for Christ

The concept of the Great Commission is found in these three passages: Matthew 28:19–20; Mark 16:15–16; and Acts 1:8. Jesus calls every believer to be involved in the work of evangelism. This assignment of witnessing for Christ should not be left for the evangelists or pastors alone (Ephesians 4:11). Instead, it is the duty of every believer to be the salt of the earth and the light of the world (Matthew 5:13–16).

The apostle Paul made an emphatic statement regarding being an effective witness for Christ: "For if I preach the gospel, I have nothing to boast of, for necessity is laid upon me; yes, woe is me if I do not preach the gospel" (1 Corinthians 9:16). And according to the apostle Peter, we must always be ready to tell others the reason for our hope in Christ. "But sanctify the Lord God in your hearts, and always be ready to give a defense to everyone who asks you the reason for the hope that is in you, with meekness and fear" (1 Peter 3:15). We all have been called to be witnesses for Christ, no matter what circumstances we find ourselves.

A Call to Follow Christ

Jesus called his disciples one by one and promised to make them fishers of men (Matthew 4:19; Mark 1:16–20). The first instruction was to follow Christ, and the second step was for him to make something out of each one of them. It is important to follow Jesus step by step in this journey of discipleship. Following entails knowing the character of the person you follow: his plans, desires, aspirations, and purpose, and how to realize them. If you follow Jesus diligently, every purpose that God has for your life will eventually be realized.

A Call to Carry Your Cross Daily and Follow Him

In Matthew 16:24–27, Jesus presented the cost of discipleship and its reward. Jesus has called all believers to carry their cross, follow him daily, and never be ashamed to suffer for Christ's sake. The apostle Paul put it this way: "But God forbid that I should boast except in the cross of our Lord Jesus Christ, by whom the world has been crucified to me, and I to the world" (Galatians 6:14). We must not be ashamed to carry the cross of Christ or suffer the reproach associated with it (Romans 1:16). Living for Christ should be a delight because of what he has already accomplished for us on the cross.

A Call to Serve One Another

In John 13:1–17, Jesus demonstrated the leader-servant attitude during a teaching moment with his disciples. The fact that he got up, laid aside his garment, took a towel, poured water into a basin, and began to wash the disciples' feet was a demonstration of humility, which the disciples would never forget. Our calling within the body of Christ is not just to enjoy the fellowship but also to serve one another. Jesus also said in Luke 22:27, "For who is greater, he who sits at the table, or he who serves? Is it not he who sits at the table? Yet I am among you as the one who serves." There is no amount of service that would be too much to render within the body of Christ.

Do you know that the call of God is upon your life? Discover what he wants you to do, how he wants you to serve, and where your primary assignment is, and you will enjoy your work with him the rest of your life.

A Call to a Life of Holiness and Peace

The Bible reminds us of the importance of holiness as we desire to walk with God. "But as He who called you is holy, you also be holy in all your conduct, because it is written, 'Be holy, for I am holy'" (1 Peter 1:15–16). We have the same instruction in Hebrews 12:14: "Pursue peace with all people, and holiness, without which no one will see the Lord." In a time when anything goes, when many people think that a life of holiness is outdated, we still need to adhere to the urgent call of holiness unto the Lord. This is paramount in our walk with God, unless heaven is not our goal.

The writer of the book of Hebrews admonished his audience to pursue peace with others and a life of holiness, because God does not use dirty vessels, but the ones that have been purified. Paul the apostle said:

> Nevertheless, the solid foundation of God stands, having this seal: The lord knows those who are His, and, let everyone who names the name of Christ depart from iniquity. But in a great house there are not only vessels of gold and of silver, but also of wood and clay, some for honor, and some for dishonor. Therefore, if a man cleanses himself from the latter, he will be a vessel for honor, sanctified and useful for the Master, prepared for every good work. (2 Timothy 2:19–21)

God uses individuals who have purified themselves and desire to abide constantly in the vine (John 15:1–16). As a disciple who looks forward to heaven, your attitude should be to submit to the leadership of the Holy Spirit throughout your life's journey.

A Call to Keep the Faith

Keeping the faith by maintaining Christian principles without compromise is of paramount importance in any given generation. Brother Jude admonished his audience to contend for what they believed: "Beloved, while I was very diligent to write to you concerning our common salvation, I found it necessary to write to you exhorting you to *content earnestly for the faith* which was once for all delivered to the saints" (Jude 3; emphasis added). The danger of false doctrine was prevalent during the first century, and Jude wanted the believers to contend for the true faith without compromising the original tenets of the Word of God. The faith that was delivered to the saints came with power to heal, save, transform, and give hope that is anchored on God himself. The apostle Paul stated clearly toward the end of his life that he had kept the faith: "I have fought the good fight, I have finished the race, I have kept the faith" (2 Timothy 4:7). Just as Paul fought gallantly during his time on earth as God's ambassador, we have been called to keep the faith, irrespective of the circumstances of our life.

A Call to Abstain from All Appearance of Evil

The apostle Paul urged the Thessalonians to "abstain from every form of evil" (1 Thessalonians 5:22). What was in Paul's mind when he said this? It means "counterfeit teaching and living should be rejected and avoided. Furthermore, as Paul broadened his warning, every form of evil should be avoided."[35] A Christian is not supposed to live an obscured life. In other words, a believer ought to live a transparent life that is evident before all people, believers and nonbelievers included. Our character speaks eloquently of what we believe and practice, and as such, we must avoid anything that would bring shame to the gospel of Christ (1 Corinthians 10:31; Colossians 3:17, 23).

A Call to Sanctification

"For this is the will of God, your *sanctification*: that ye should abstain from sexual immorality; that each of you should know how to possess his vessel in *sanctification* and honor" (1 Thessalonians 4:3–4; emphasis added). What is sanctification? According to Ronald F. Youngblood and coauthors, sanctification is "the process of God's grace by which the believer is separated from sin and becomes dedicated to God's righteousness."[36] Sanctification is the act or process of acquiring sanctity or being made or becoming holy. To sanctify something is to literally set it apart for a particular use in a special purpose, because the thing being set apart is holy or sacred.

According to the above passage (1 Thessalonians 4:3–4), sanctification is the will of God for all believers; therefore, it is not an

---

[35] John F. Walvood and Roy B. Zuck, *The Bible Knowledge Commentary: New Testament; And Exposition of the Scriptures by Dallas Seminary* (Colorado Springs: Chariot Victor Publishing, 1983) 709.

[36] Ronal F. Youngblood, F. F. Bruce, and R. K. Harrison; *New Illustrated Bible Dictionary: Completely Revised and Updated Edition* (Nashville, TN: Thomas Nelson Publishers, 1995) 1126.

option or suggestion, but a command from the Lord to which all of us should strictly adhere. It is God's desire that believers should possess their vessels in honor. The word *vessel* refers to the body, which is the temple of the Holy Spirit (1 Corinthians 6:19–20), and which Jesus purchased with his blood on the cross.

According to the apostle Paul in 1 Thessalonians 4:3–4, the call to sanctification is also related to abstaining from fornication. What is fornication? It means any unlawful sexual relationship, including adultery. Fornication means committing an illicit sexual union or having a sexual relationship with someone not married to you. We are living in the age of sexual revolution, when people regard biblical principles on sexual issues as outdated. Whether we believe it or not, abstinence for the unmarried is still the best. But those who are married should be faithful to their partners. Of course, we see the consequences of unfaithful marital relationships in the world around us, as people contract incurable diseases by having multiple partners. God has called us to be good stewards of our bodies by conducting ourselves with sanctity and honor. Remember, we cannot escape the law of nature, for whatever people sow is what they will harvest eventually (Galatians 6:7–8).

CHAPTER 3

Biblical Foundations of Discipleship

We shall examine the issues of discipleship from a biblical perspective in order to lay a solid foundation that is anchored by Jesus's teachings on the subject. In the process, we shall look into the works of Bible scholars who have done extensive research on Christian discipleship.

Who Is a Disciple?

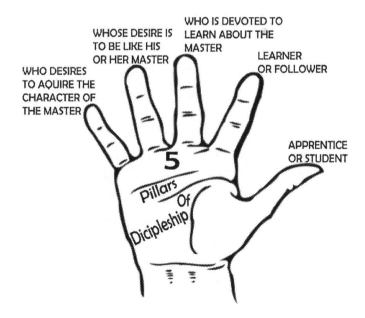

According to David Watson, "The word disciple meant an apprentice in some trade, a student of some subject, or a pupil of some trade."[37] Jeffrey Jones states, "Two words that are particularly important for our understanding are learner and follower. That a disciple is a learner—he or she wants to learn more about the teachings and ways of life of a particular person."[38] Furthermore, according to Jones, "The disciple wants to do more than learn; the disciple also wants to follow … and it is through following that the disciple learns."[39]

Disciples study under their masters, and their ultimate purpose is to be like them. For us, our purpose and aspiration is to be like Jesus in character. A disciple is a follower—one who accepts and assists in spreading the doctrines of another. A Christian disciple is a person who accepts and assists in the spreading of the good news of Jesus Christ. Christian discipleship is the process by which disciples grow in the Lord Jesus Christ and are equipped by the Holy Spirit, who resides in our hearts, to overcome the pressures and trials of this present life and become more and more Christlike. This process requires believers to respond to the Holy Spirit's prompting to examine their thoughts, words, and actions and compare them with the Word of God. This requires that we be in the Word daily: studying it, praying over it, and obeying it. In addition, we should always be ready to give testimony of the reason for the hope that is within us (1 Peter 3:15) and to disciple others to walk in his way.

A disciple is "a follower of Jesus Christ in his lifetime; one who accepts and assists in spreading the doctrine of another, for example as one of the twelve in the inner circle of Christ's followers in the Gospel account; a convinced adherent of a school or individual; a follower."[40] Disciples are people who follow after the steps of their master. According to David Watson, "Discipleship means knowing

---

[37] David Watson, *Called & Committed: World-Changing Discipleship* (Wheaton, IL: Harold Shaw, 1989), 5.

[38] Jeffrey D. Jones, *Traveling Together: A Guide for Disciple-Forming Congregations* (Lanham, MD: Rowman & Littlefield, 2006), 40.

[39] Ibid., 41.

[40] *Merriam-Webster's Collegiate Dictionary*, s.v. "disciple."

Jesus, loving him, believing in him, and being committed to him."[41] In a Christian context, the entering point of disciples is when they encounter Jesus Christ and accept him as Lord and Savior.

Discipleship from Jesus's Perspective

A call to discipleship from Jesus's perspective is a call to forsake all, deny oneself, take up the cross, and follow him. The scripture records in Luke 14:25–27, 33:

> Now great multitudes went with Him. And He turned and said to them, if anyone comes to Me and does not hate his father and mother, wife and children, brothers and sisters, yes, and his own life also, he cannot be My disciple. And whoever does not bear his cross and come after Me cannot be My disciple … so likewise, whoever of you does not forsake all that he has cannot be My disciple.

What does it really mean to hate oneself or one's family as the cost of discipleship? Was Jesus advocating for hatred toward one's family? The answer is no. Instead, Jesus in the above context taught that a Christian's devotedness to Jesus should take precedence over all other relationships. This can be seen as a clear exaggeration that, in a real sense, means less love toward our natural relationships compared to the love we express toward Christ. Jesus illustrated the principle that divine love is greater than natural affection when he made reference to his family:

> Then one said to Him, "Look, Your mother and Your brothers are standing outside, seeking to speak with You." But He answered and said to the one who told Him, "Who is My mother and who are My brothers?" And He stretched out His hand toward His disciples and said, "Here are My mother and My brothers. For

---

[41] Watson, *Called & Committed*, 9.

whoever does the will of My Father in heaven is My brother and sister and mother." (Matthew 12:47–50)

The lesson from the above passage is that Jesus wants his disciples to love God even more than their immediate family. David Watson noted an important aspect of discipleship: the pain or suffering associated with ministry. Watson said, "Discipleship is never easy; often it involves pain and tears, when we shall have to rethink our values and our ambition to follow Christ. But we are not called to face this challenge on our own."[42] With regard to the joy and pain associated with ministry, Jeffrey Jones says,

> I dislike pain and conflict as much as anyone, and yet I have learned that ministry often involves both of these. I have also learned that it is in these times that the depth of relationship with God, self, and others in community, the awareness of our gifts, and the clarity of our call are crucially important.[43]

We can add that emotional pain in ministry is not new, as we can see in the words of the apostle Paul in his letter to Timothy as he was awaiting his execution:

> Be diligent to come to me quickly; for Demas has forsaken me, having loved the present world, and has departed for Thessalonica—Crescens for Galatia, Titus for Dalmatia. Luke is with me. Get Mark and bring him with you, for he is very useful to me for ministry. And Tychicus I have sent to Ephesus. Bring the cloak that I left with Carpus at Troas when you come—and the books, especially the parchments. Alexander the coppersmith did me much harm. May the Lord repay him according to his works. You also must beware of

---

[42] Ibid.
[43] Jones, *Traveling Together,* 61–62.

him, for he has greatly resisted our words. (2 Timothy
4:9–15)

The expression of Paul in the above passage was that of abandonment
by Demas, who had left the ministry because of worldly affairs. Paul
longed to see Timothy, probably because his days were numbered
(2 Timothy 4:6–8). Watson writes further, "Suffering is inescapably
woven into the fabric of discipleship—'joy and woe are woven fine,'
wrote William Blake. But it is in suffering that God is working most
profoundly in our lives."[44] Suffering for the sake of the gospel should
not discourage us because Jesus had earlier made it clear that those who
want to be his disciples must take up their cross daily and follow him.
Watson says:

> The call to obey, to serve, to live a simple lifestyle,
> to suffer and, if need be, to die, is common to all
> followers of Jesus. Above all, we are to commit our lives
> unreservedly to him and to one another as members of
> his body. The Christian Church is not a club that we
> belong to so that our needs will be met; it is a body, a
> building, a family, an army; by accepting the call of
> Christ, we take on responsibility that we cannot avoid
> if we are to be his disciple.[45]

Our call to discipleship is a call to obedience, just as Jesus said, "You
are My friends if you do what I command you" (John 15:14). Watson
says,

> To obey God's will is to find the fulfillment of our
> lives … to follow him, to go the way that he goes, to
> accept his plan for our lives; it is a call to say no to the

---

[44] Watson, *Called & Committed*, 15.
[45] Ibid., 16.

old life of sin, and to say yes to Jesus … there is no true
faith and no true discipleship without obedience.[46]

Jesus must be the Lord in all aspects of our lives, and if he is not, then the implication is that we have not surrendered totally to him. Watson says, "If Christ is not Lord of all, he is not Lord at all. It is impossible to be a partial disciple of Jesus."[47] We must be willing to make him the Lord over all our possessions in order to experience the inner tranquility that the world cannot understand. "The decision to become a disciple of Jesus of Nazareth meant taking an unqualified risk, a willingness to abandon everything the world held to be important for the sake of those things that were of eternal importance."[48] The gospel is associated with pain, suffering, persecution, and even death, but no amount of discouragement or intimidation will stop the propagation of the Word of God. The present suffering cannot be compared with the glory that will be revealed in us (Romans 8:18). Speaking on the issue of suffering, Robert E. Coleman said,

> Many would suffer persecution and martyrdom in
> the battle. Yet no matter how great the trials through
> which his people would pass, and how many temporal
> skirmishes were lost in the struggle, the ultimate victory
> was certain. His church would win in the end.[49]

Nobody said it would be an easy task to spread the good news. Even Jesus said that the world will hate us (Matthew 10:22; Mark 13:13; Luke 21:17). The apostle Paul told Timothy to endure hardship as a good soldier of Jesus Christ (2 Timothy 2:3).

What does it really mean to make disciples? According to Coleman:

---

[46] Ibid., 7.

[47] Ibid., 10.

[48] David Watson, *Covenant Discipleship: Christian Formation through Mutual Accountability* (Nashville, TN: Discipleship Resource Publications, 1989), 2.

[49] Robert E. Coleman; *The Master Plan of Evangelism* (Grand Rapids, MI: Baker, 1993), 98.

These three words, *go*, *baptize* and *teach* are all participles which derive their force from the one controlling verb, "make disciples." This means that the Great Commission is not merely to go to the ends of the earth preaching the gospel (Mark 16:15), nor baptize a lot of converts into the name of the triune God, not to teach the precepts of Christ, but to "make disciples" to build people like themselves, who were so constrained by the commission of Christ that they not only followed, but also led others to follow his way.[50]

In fact, discipleship is about preservation and transmission of godly principles that we have learned ourselves. In other words, unless we have taken time to learn properly, we will not be able to positively influence the succeeding generation. That was the kind of discipleship pattern advocated by apostle Paul in 2 Timothy 2:2: "And the things that you have heard from me among many witnesses, commit these to faithful men who will be able to teach others also" There is a spiritual chain reaction of discipleship that follows this instruction, because Paul expected Timothy to take the divine revelation he had learned from him and teach it to faithful followers, who would in turn pass it on to others with proven character, who would entrust the scriptural truths to the next generation. We see both in the Old and New Testaments the same process of discipleship. For example, Moses influenced Joshua, Elijah influenced Elisha, Jesus influenced the twelve disciples, Ananias influenced Paul (Acts 9:11–19), and Paul influenced Timothy, Titus, Onesimus, and so on. Our work with the new converts within our congregations ought to follow the same pattern. Unless we live out godly principles for others to see, we might not adequately influence the incoming generation.

---

[50] Ibid., 101.

Conclusion

The acceptance of the lordship of Christ over one's life is the beginning of discipleship. Growing in Christ is a process of deepening our relationships, both vertically and horizontally. In other words, vertical relationship that connects us with God will eventually affect the horizontal relationships we have with other people around us. Discipleship does not happen in isolation but within the context of a community.

According to Jones, "It is community that offers the experiences of deepening, equipping and ministering that forms disciples."[51] In other words, the essential factors for nurturing a disciple could be said to be confined within the local church, where adequate resources, significant pastoral care, learning about the Bible, prayer, evangelism, and the development of spiritual disciplines are provided. This involves active participation of members as they fulfill their callings by reaching out to new believers and nonbelievers alike, with the goal of discipleship.

Discipleship involves the reproduction of our faith in others, who will continue the propagation of the gospel. According to Coleman,

> Christ's whole evangelistic strategy—indeed, the fulfillment of his very purpose in coming into the world, dying on the cross, and rising from the grave—depended on the faithfulness of his chosen disciples to this task. It did not matter how small the group was to start with so long as they reproduced and taught their disciples to reproduce.[52]

In essence, Coleman is advocating that believers live in such a manner that they can influence others through their lifestyle. That is one of the ways we can spread the good news of Jesus Christ within our community.

---

[51] Ibid., 65.
[52] Ibid., 99.

The Principles of Christian Discipleship

According to J. Lee Grady, there are six Is involved in the process of Christian discipleship: Identify, Invest, Include, Instruct, Intercede, and Impart.[53]

PRINCIPLES OF CHRISTIAN DISCIPLESHIP

Identify

This is the act of identifying someone with the purpose of maintaining a close relationship, so that the person would be imparted positively. In other words, it is important to identify those you will invest in. It could be your children, staff, colleagues, church elders, or friends who are hungry for the things of Lord.

Invest

Investing involves the act of endowing with quality for a future benefit. To invest here means the act of imparting spiritual investment in the lives of those who seem interested in the things of God. What you offer is your time, which could be a one-on-one conversation, a small group, or a bigger group. For example, Jesus had a group of seventy disciples: "After these things the Lord appointed seventy others also and

---

[53] J. Lee Grady, "Six Principles of Christian Discipleship," presentation at International Fellowship of Christian Assemblies Convention, August 5–7, 2015, Sandusky, Ohio.

sent them two by two before His face into every city and place where He Himself was about to go" (Luke 10:1). He also had twelve disciples: "And when He had called His twelve disciples to Him, He gave them power over unclean spirits, to cast them out, and to heal all kinds of sickness and all kinds of disease" (Matthew 10:1).

Jesus also had three disciples who belonged to the inner group: "Now after six days Jesus took Peter, James and John his brother, led them up on a high mountain by themselves" (Matthew 17:1). Whatever investment you make in the lives of disciples will eventually come back to you in the form of rewards or blessings. Deliberate attempt should be made to influence the new converts, either in a small or large group setting, just as we learn from Jesus's model.

Include

To include in the context of discipleship means to make a deliberate arrangement for a new convert to participate in your programs. Inclusion means involvement with the intention of influencing someone positively toward Christlikeness. In terms of discipleship or ministry, you must make a deliberate attempt to include the younger generation for the purpose of propagating the gospel. The apostle Paul said to Timothy, "And the things you have heard from Me among many witnesses, commit these to faithful men who will be able to teach others also" (2 Timothy 2:2).

From Paul's perspective, Timothy should identify reliable people among the believers who would be taught godly principles, and these people should be qualified to instruct others also. It is paramount to include those you want to disciple in your mission trips, vacation, or camp meeting. If possible, allow them to participate actively during your preaching engagements.

Instruct

To instruct means to pass knowledge to someone else, especially as related to the knowledge of the scripture, which is important to the spiritual growth of new converts. It is important to instruct new converts toward pursuing God's righteousness:

> All scripture is given by inspiration of God, and is profitable for doctrine, for reproof, for correction, for instruction in righteousness, that the man of God may be complete, thoroughly equipped for every good work. (2 Timothy 3:16–17)

The instruction from God's Word provides stability, faith in the true Lord, guidance, and direction in path of righteousness (Psalm 119:105). Here are some passages that talk about instruction and its benefits:

- "Listen to counsel and receive instruction that you may be wise in your latter days" (Proverbs 19:20).
- "I will instruct you and teach you in the way you should go; I will guide you with My eye" (Psalm 32:8).
- "Take firm hold of instruction, do not let go; keep her, for she is your life" (Proverbs 4:13).

Instruction in God's Word is important in discipleship because, through it, the life of the disciple is imparted positively.

Intercede

This means to plead on behalf of someone else. However, in discipleship, we are called to pray and lift up before God the people we disciple, especially when we are not with them. We can equally send emails and text messages, write letters, or make phone calls just to demonstrate that we care for them. The apostle Paul prayed for spiritual growth on behalf of the Ephesian and Colossian churches, and these prayers are examples of how we should pray for our disciples (Ephesians 3:14–21; Colossians 1:9–14). Paul's desire was that Jesus be formed in their lives: "My little children, for whom I labor in birth again until

Christ is formed in you" (Galatians 4:19). We are encouraged to pray until our prayers have influenced the people we disciple.

Impart

This means to communicate or convey something tangible. In discipleship, it could mean to give spiritual gifts. For example, the apostle Paul's desire was to impart spiritual gifts upon believers in Rome: "For I long to see you, that I may impart to you some spiritual gift, so that you may be established" (Romans 1:11). Moses imparted his mission to Joshua. Elijah imparted his authority to Elisha and later threw his mantle upon him. Elijah's passage of responsibility to Elisha was so visible that he had a fruitful ministry. Jesus imparted the gospel to the twelve disciples, who later made such a great impact on the world around them that it was reported that they turned the world upside down (Acts 17:6). It is our responsibility to impart discipleship principles to the incoming generation in order for them to make a positive change in their own time.

Becoming a Reproducing, Disciple-Making Congregation

Robert Coleman's *Master Plan of Evangelism* describes eight principles paramount to reproducing quality disciples within Christendom.[54] These principles are selection, association, consecration, impartation, demonstration, delegation, supervision, and reproduction.

These principles from Coleman are important in discipleship; however, we need to know that not all of them are applicable in every Christian discipleship program. Nevertheless, one may ask, how do we apply these principles to the discipleship process? Following are some helpful discussions on the aforementioned principles from Coleman.

---

[54] Robert E. Coleman. *The Master Plan of Evangelism* (Grand Rapids, MI: Baker Book House, 1993) 27.

ROBERT COLEMANS MASTER PLAN FOR DISCIPLESHIP

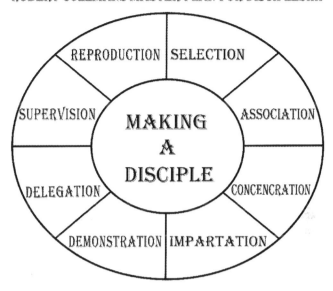

Selection

This is the act or process of choosing people to be discipled. Jesus gave us examples in the way he selected his initial disciples. He was the one who made the choice and not the disciples. The disciples did not campaign to be selected and did not merit it on their own terms. It was solely dependent on Christ's judgment to select who he wanted (John 15:16). We can equally look through our congregation and choose certain individuals with the purpose of discipling them.

According to Coleman, "The initial objective of Jesus' plan was to enlist men who could bear witness to his life and carry on his work after he returned to the Father."[55] "And Jesus, walking by the Sea of Galilee, saw two brothers, Simon called Peter, and Andrew, his brother, casting a net into the sea; for they were fishermen. Then He said to them, 'Follow Me, and I will make you fishers of men'" (Matthew 4:18–19). The Master also called the sons of Zebedee, who were also fishermen, and they left their nets and followed him (Matthew 4:21–22). Jesus also called Matthew the tax collector to follow him (Matthew 9:9–13). The

---

[55] Ibid., 27.

key principle in this selection process is that Jesus is the one who makes disciples. When we heed to the call to follow him, we accept everything, including responsibility that goes with it, whether good or bad, whether joy or suffering, whether gain or loss, life or death.

Matthew stated that Jesus called unto him the twelve disciples, whose names are mentioned in Matthew 10:2–4. The twelve men he selected became his students, who were empowered by the Master to bring positive change in the world around them.

Association

This is the act of establishing a relationship or bond between individuals, with the purpose of having a common interest. According to Robert Coleman, in this association process, "Jesus had no formal school, no seminaries, no outline course of study, no periodic membership classes in which he enrolled his followers."[56] We can infer that discipleship occurred as those selected had association with Jesus Christ, even though there was no formal curriculum or classroom setting. The time they spent with Jesus influenced their lives tremendously, and this radical informal training was what they needed to fulfill the ministry to which they were called.

Consecration

This is the act of dedicating to the service of God the people who have been called by the Master. Jesus demanded absolute obedience as he called them into this sacred office (John 15:1–16). It is a call to submit totally to the requirements of the Master. Disciples are learners; therefore, the process requires submission and obedience to the core. It seems the disciples understood the importance of their calling, and later in their journey of discipleship, they reached the point of being willing to die for what they believed.

---

[56] Ibid., 41.

Following Jesus seemed easy enough at first, but that was because they had not followed him very far. It soon became apparent that being a disciple of Christ involved far more than a joyful acceptance of the Messianic promise: it meant the surrender of one's whole life to the Master in absolute submission to his sovereignty.[57]

As disciples of Jesus, we must be willing to submit to him and obey him in order to have a fruitful and meaningful ministry.

Impartation

Impartation involves the process of communicating or conveying the truth of God's Word to the learner or disciple. Having understood the mission of the Master, they were willing to evangelize the world around them by telling the story of the risen Savior.

Jesus gave his life away, not only to the disciples, but also to the whole world (John 3:16). His impact on the lives of his disciples was evident in the way they turned the world upside down (Acts 17:6). The apostle Paul also knew the importance of impartation, as he expressed in his letter to the believers in Rome: "For I long to see you, that I may impart to you some spiritual gift, so that you may be established" (Romans 1:11). With the impartation of spiritual gifts, the church in Rome would be more equipped to do ministry and thereby to influence the world, since Rome drew visitors from throughout the empire.

To what extent did Jesus impart his mission to his disciples? Coleman says,

> He gave them the keys to his kingdom against which the powers of hell could never prevail (Matt. 16:19; Luke 12:32). Indeed, he gave them his own glory which was his before the worlds were made, that they all might be one even as he was one in the Father (John 17:22,

---

[57] Ibid., 52.

24). He gave all he had—nothing was withheld, not even his own life.[58]

In fact, Jesus's impact on the disciples was so significant that the followers in Antioch were called Christians for the first time (Acts 11:26). This implies that they resembled Christ in their conduct and attitude.

Demonstration

Demonstration is the act of showing through practical examples what new converts ought to know as regards to the job they have been called into. For example, Jesus sent out the disciples two by two for the purpose of evangelization (Mark 6:7). They also saw his prayer life, which he demonstrated often before them. In fact, that was a typical example on-the-job training. In Jesus's work of discipleship through demonstration, Robert Coleman states,

> He showed them how to live.... Jesus saw to it that his disciples learned his way of living with God and man.... Take, for example, his prayer life. Surely it was no accident that Jesus often let his disciples see him conversing with the Father.[59]

Jesus presented practical aspects of learning through modeling. No wonder he made so great an impact in the lives of his disciples within a space of three years in earthly ministry. They learned how to pray by watching him (Luke 1:1–13) and learned how to evangelize as they were sent out two by two (Mark 6:7; Luke 10:1).

> They observed how he drew people to himself; how he won their confidence and inspired their faith; how he opened to them the way of salvation and called them to

---

[58] Ibid., 61–62.
[59] Ibid., 71.

a decision. In all types of situations and among all kinds of people, rich and poor, healthy and sick, friend and foe alike, the disciples watched the master soul-winner at work.[60]

Indeed, Jesus demonstrated the work in their presence, and when he departed, they jumped into the work after the outpouring of the Holy Spirit (Acts 2). The impact of the Master's life on them was evident as they affected the world with the good news of the Gospel.

Delegation

This is the act of empowering another person to carry out a responsibility, with the expectation that the work will be done accurately. Jesus delegated responsibilities to his disciples, which they carried out to his satisfaction.

> He assigned them work.… Jesus was always building his ministry for the time when his disciples would have to take over his work and go out into the world with the redeeming gospel. This plan was progressively made clear as they followed him.[61]

The task before them was to preach the kingdom of God, to baptize those who believed, and to heal the sick (Matthew 10:1, 28:19–20; Mark 6:7; Luke 9:1). Jesus also instructed them to "heal the sick, cleanse the lepers, raise the dead, cast out demons" (Matthew 10:8). The disciples were happy at the outcome of their outreach, but Jesus told them not to rejoice because spirits submitted to them; instead, they should rejoice because their names were written in the book of life (Luke 10:20). It was through delegation that the disciples learned on the job and were able to spread the gospel that transformed the world after Jesus ascended to heaven. We can learn from this principle by delegating appropriate

[60] Ibid., 74–75.
[61] Ibid., 79.

responsibilities to new converts as we disciple them and as they mature in their relationship with Christ.

Supervision

This is the process of watching people and directing them to do what is appropriate. For example, it is the responsibility of the supervisor to direct other employees to carry out the policy of the organization within the job setting. Jesus supervised his disciples during their day-to-day activities, providing direct guidance. His supervisory method provided a model for the disciples to adopt after Jesus had returned to heaven. Jesus maintained close contact with them, as he gave them both instruction and assignments. He also expected feedback from the disciples. For example, the seventy who were sent out came back with reports that demons were subject to them during their mission outreach (Luke 10:17).

Stressing the importance of Jesus's close contact with his disciples, Coleman stated,

> What time he was with them, he was helping them to understand the reason for some previous action or getting them ready for some new experience. His questions, illustrations, warnings, and admonitions were calculated to bring out those things that they needed to know in order to fulfill his work, which was the evangelization of the world.[62]

Jesus was focused on his supervisory role, making sure that the disciples understood their responsibilities and achieved results. Coleman noted,

> He would not let them rest in success or failure. No matter what they did, there was always more to do and to learn. He rejoiced in their success, but nothing less

---

[62] Ibid., 89.

than world conquest was his goal, and to that end he always superintended their efforts.[63]

As we disciple others, it is important to provide the necessary supervision that will enable new converts and other believers to reach their goals in life as they follow their own callings.

Reproduction

This is the "act or process of reproducing; the process by which plants and animals give rise to offspring and which fundamentally consist of the segregation of a portion of the parental body by a sexual or an asexual process and its subsequent growth and differentiation into a new individual."[64] Reproduction is the ability of trees or animals to reproduce their own kind. But in the spiritual sense, Jesus expects his disciples to reproduce by winning souls into the kingdom of God.

What does Jesus expect from his disciples? According to Coleman,

> Jesus intended for the disciples to produce his likeness in and through the church being gathered out of the world. Thus his ministry in the Spirit would be duplicated many-fold by his ministry in the lives of his disciples. Through them and others like them it would continue to expand in an ever-enlarging circumference until the multitudes might know in a similar way the opportunity which they had known with the Master. By this strategy the conquest of the world was only a matter of time and their faithfulness to his plan.[65]

Jesus stressed the importance of fruitfulness as he taught his disciples about the true vine in John 15. The secret of reproduction is for the branch to abide in the main tree. Jesus expected his disciples

---

[63] Ibid., 93.
[64] *Merriam-Webster's Collegiate Dictionary*, s.v. "reproduction."
[65] Coleman, *The Master Plan of Evangelism*, 97.

then, and those of today, to constantly remain in him for nourishment and fruitfulness. His ultimate purpose of choosing his disciples in every generation is to bear fruit that will remain (John 15:16). Bearing fruit in the above context is similar to being productive in an evangelistic outreach and harvest of souls.

> His whole evangelistic strategy—indeed, the fulfillment of his very purpose in coming into the world, dying on the cross, and rising from the grave—depended on the faithfulness of his chosen disciples to this task. It did not matter how small the group was to start with so long as they reproduced and taught their disciples to reproduce. This was the way his church was to win—through the dedicated lives of those who knew the Savior so well that his Spirit and method constrained them to tell others. As simple as it may seem, this was the way the gospel would conquer. He had no other plan.[66]

Robert Coleman's eight principles of evangelism and discipleship serve as a strategy for helping new converts to mature in their Christian faith. Undoubtedly, these principles, if applied appropriately, will help to nurture new converts to Christianity.

---

[66] Ibid., 99.

CHAPTER 4

Walking in the Power of the Holy Spirit

That which is born of the flesh is flesh, and that which is born of the Spirit is spirit.

—John 3:6

The Power of the Holy Spirit in the Life of a Believer

For many centuries, there has been serious and unending controversy about the person of the Holy Spirit. The Holy Spirit, who is the third person in the Triune God, has been at work right from the beginning of creation (Gen. 1:1–2). According to the scriptures, he is the

- Spirit of God and of Christ (Matthew 3:16; 2 Corinthians 3:17; 1 Peter 1:11);
- breath of life (Genesis 2:7; Ezekiel 37:9–10);
- revealer of truth (John 14:17, 16:13; Luke 2:26: 1 Corinthians 2:12–16);
- harmonizer, illuminator, teacher of truth, and guardian (John 14:26, 16:13; 1 Corinthians 2:13);
- confirmer (Acts 10:1–5, 9–22; 13:1–3);
- giver of spiritual gifts (Romans 12:3–8; 1 Corinthians 12:1–14);
- instructor, comforter or helper, counselor, advocate (John 14:16, 26, 16:7; Isaiah 11:2);

- revealer of sinful lifestyle (John 16:7–8);
- life giver (Romans 8:2, 11);
- witness (Romans 8:16);
- intercessor (Romans 8:26);
- indweller of believers (Romans 8:9–16; Ephesians 2:21–22; 1 Corinthians 6:19);
- author of scriptures (2 Timothy 3:16; 2 Peter 1:21); and
- deposit and seal guaranteeing the believer's salvation (2 Corinthians 1:22, 5:5; Ephesians 1:13–14).

Jesus recognized the importance of the Holy Spirit in the life of his disciples, and he instructed them to wait until they were endowed with power from on high (Luke 24:47). The Holy Spirit played an important role in the life of Jesus himself: in his birth (Matthew 1:18–20; Luke 1:34–35); at his baptism (Matthew 3:16); giving him power to overcome temptation (Matthew 4:1–11); in his resurrection (Romans 8:11); and anointing him to heal the sick and fulfill his ministry (Acts 10:38; Matthew 4:23, 8:16, 9:35, 15:30; Luke 4:40).

As a new covert to Christ in the late 1970s, I grew up in an environment where some Christian leaders deemphasized the importance of the Holy Spirit in the life of a believer. I subscribed to that idea at the time but later became associated with members of the Scripture Union and a Bible-believing church. I learned from them that I cannot live a victorious Christian life without the power of the Holy Spirit. Immediately, I embraced the uncompromised, undiluted teaching of the Bible, and I was baptized in the Holy Spirit with the evidence of speaking in tongues. This instantly changed my life, and since then, I have benefited so much from the leadership of the Holy Spirit.

One may ask what I mean by the evidence of speaking in tongues. This concept is biblical from three passages in the book of Acts:

> When the Day of Pentecost had fully come, they were all with one accord in one place. And suddenly there came a sound from heaven, as of a rushing mighty wind, and it filled the whole house where they were

sitting. Then there appeared to them divided tongues, as of fire, and one sat upon each of them. And they were all filled with the Holy Spirit and began to speak with other tongues, as the Spirit gave them utterance. (Acts 2:1–4)

Occurrences in two other passages in the book of Acts also justify the claim that it is important to believe the totality of the scripture rather than human doctrines.

While Peter was still speaking these words, the Holy Spirit fell upon those who heard the word. And those of the circumcision who believed were astonished, as many as came with Peter, because the gift of the Holy Spirit has been poured out on the Gentiles also. For they heard them speak with tongues and magnify God. (Acts 10:44–46)

And it happened, while Apollos was at Corinth, that Paul, having passed through the upper regions, came to Ephesus. And finding some disciples he said to them, "Did you receive the Holy Spirit when you believed?" so they said to him, "We have not so much as heard whether there is a Holy Spirit." And he said to them, "Into what then were you baptized?" So they said, "Into John's baptism." Then Paul said, "John indeed baptized with a baptism of repentance, saying to the people that they should believe on Him who would come after him, that is on Christ Jesus." When they heard this, they were baptized in the name of the Lord Jesus. And when Paul had laid hands on them, the Holy Spirit came upon them, and they spoke with tongues and prophesied. (Acts 19:1–6)

We can see from these three passages (Acts 2:1–4; 10:44–46; 19:1–6) that speaking in tongues is the evidence of the infilling of the Holy Spirit. It is high time we declare the uncompromised and undiluted Word of God rather than believing human reasoning that is at variance with the Word of God. The apostle Paul, who believed in declaring the whole counsel of God (Acts 20:27), said he spoke in tongues more than anyone, as he testified to the Corinthian church (1 Corinthians 14:18).

It is vital that a Bible-based teaching on the person of the Holy Spirit be presented to new believers right from the outset in order for them to embrace the Holy Spirit, who will empower and energize them throughout their discipleship (and, of course, their entire lives).

The discussion in this booklet includes practical examples to substantiate the role of the Holy Spirit in the lives of people in the Old and New Testaments who walked with God.

For example, God put the Spirit on Moses and also on seventy elders:

> Then the Lord came down in a cloud, and spoke to him, and took of the Spirit that was upon him, and placed the same upon the seventy elders; and it happened, when the Spirit rested upon them, that they prophesied, although they never did so again. (Numbers 11:25)

The Spirit of God upon the seventy elders was to empower them for fruitful endeavors as they assisted Moses in the work of the Lord.

Similarly, Samson was empowered by God's Spirit right from the womb, to carry out mighty things as Israel's deliverer (Judges 13:1–5). He uprooted the gate of the enemy and took it to the hill (Judges 16:1–3) and singlehandedly used a jawbone of a donkey to kill a thousand Philistines (Judges 15:14–16). He recognized that he was not an ordinary person, even as he foolishly revealed the secret of his power:

> And it came to pass, when she pestered him daily with her words and pressed him, so that his soul was vexed to death, that he told her all his heart, and said to

her, no razor has ever come upon my head, for I have
been a Nazirite to God from my mother's womb. If
I am shaven, then my strength will leave me, and I
shall become weak, and *be like any other man* (Judges
16:16–17; emphasis added).

Samson recognized that he was not an ordinary man because of the
Holy Spirit in him. Likewise, every believer must recognize this fact
when the Holy Spirit rests upon them.

Saul, the first king of Israel, heard of the Spirit when he encountered
the prophet Samuel for the first time: "Then the Spirit of the Lord
will come upon you, and you will prophesy with them and *be turned
into another man*" (1 Samuel 10:6; emphasis added). We can see from
Numbers 11:25 and 1 Samuel 10:6 that the Spirit of God in the life of
a believer makes a big difference and that prophecy is the fruit of the
Spirit of God. In other words, those who are filled by the Spirit of the
living God will not only speak in tongues but also prophesy.

There are certain clear instructions about the Holy Spirit:

- "I say then: Walk in the Spirit, and you shall not fulfill the lust
  of the flesh" (Galatians 5:16).
- "And do not grieve the Holy Spirit of God, by whom you were
  sealed for the day of redemption" (Ephesians 4:30).
- "Do not quench the Spirit" (1 Thessalonians 5:19).

Samson grieved the Holy Spirit, who later left him (Judges 16:20).
Saul grieved the Holy Spirit through a life of constant disobedience,
and he was rejected as king (1 Samuel 13:8–14; 15:1–29). Today, many
of us do certain things without consulting the Holy Spirit, and we
pay heavily for the consequences of our actions. To quench the Holy
Spirit is to walk in darkness, which is fruitless (that is, without aim and
direction). Believers in Christ should not see themselves as ordinary
people, especially as they are now possessed by the Holy Spirit. "Now
may the God of peace Himself sanctify you completely; and may your
whole spirit, soul, and body be preserved blameless at the coming of

our Lord Jesus Christ" (1 Thessalonians 5:23). That was apostle Paul's prayer and desire for brethren in Thessalonica as they awaited the Second Coming of Christ. May we diligently and expectantly wait for the Lord's return.

Humans are spiritual beings, made up of body and soul. The body is the vehicle that moves one around. On the other hand, cosmic powers exist that are set against humankind (Ephesians 6:10–18). We cannot face the enemy successfully without being in the Spirit. Paul recounted his experience of trying to overcome his sinful nature but being unable to do so until he cried out to God for help (Romans 7:1–25). Later, he embraced life in the spirit and had victory (Romans 8:1–39). Romans 7 and 8 emphasize that the Holy Spirit delivers believers from the old nature by producing a life of righteousness. When someone dies, the spirit departs. The spirit gives life to the body. We are spiritual beings, having a soul and living in the body. Jesus said, "It is the Spirit who gives life; the flesh profits nothing. The words that I speak to you are spirit, and they are life" (John 6:63).

In Genesis 1:1–3, the earth was without form until the Spirit hovered over the surface of the earth. Then God spoke, and things began to happen. If God waited for the Spirit to move upon the earth before he spoke, then we must wait for the move of the Holy Spirit before we can take any action. Jesus told his disciples to tarry in Jerusalem until they were endued with the Holy Spirit (Luke 24:49). In other words, it is important to be guided and inspired by the Holy Spirit so we can do the right thing, as we minister life to the people of God. Yes, we ought to speak as God's oracle (1 Peter 4:11).

The Lord spoke light into existence through the power of the Holy Spirit (Genesis 1:3), and the apostle John pointed out that the light at the beginning of creation was Jesus Christ (John 1:1–10). Jesus was the Word that became flesh and dwelt among us, full of grace and truth (John 1:14). Jesus was baptized in the River Jordan, where the Holy Spirit officially descended on him, and the same Holy Spirit led him into the wilderness to be tempted by the devil. Jesus was not led by human reasoning, emotion, logic, feeling, philosophy, or argument, but by the Holy Spirit. He had victory over the devil because he was led by the Holy Spirit. What makes you think that you can overcome Satan without the power or leading of the Holy Spirit? Satan, the old serpent (Revelation 20:2), is wiser than humankind, but we can overcome him—not with willpower or logic, but by the power of the Holy Spirit, the blood, and our testimony (Revelation 12:11).

The Lord said, "Not by might, not by power, but by my Spirit" (Zechariah 4:6). God gives understanding to believers through his Spirit: "But there is a spirit in man, and the breath of the Almighty gives him understanding" (Job 32:8). God communicates directly to the spirit in humans when he wants to give instruction. In other words, you can know about things before they happen when you are attuned to the Spirit of God. You must be operating on the same frequency as the Holy Spirit before you can receive guidance from God, because the Holy Spirit reveals secrets and also knows the mind of God to guide and intercede for the believer (1 Corinthians 2:11; Romans 8:27). "The secret things belong to the Lord our God, but those things which are revealed belong to us and to our children forever, that we may do all the words of this law" (Deuteronomy 29:29). "Surely the Lord God does nothing, unless He reveals His secret to His servants the prophets" (Amos 3:7). A child of God who is filled with the Holy Spirit and always connected to him will receive manifold revelations.

The apostle Paul, who taught so much about the Holy Spirit and spiritual gifts, was indeed connected to the Lord.

- "Now the Lord spoke to Paul in the night by a vision, 'Do not be afraid, but speak, and do not keep silent. For I am with you, and no one will attack you to hurt you; for I have many people in this city'" (Acts 18:9–10).
- "But the following night the Lord stood by him and said, 'Be of good cheer, Paul; for as you have testified for Me in Jerusalem, so you must also bear witness at Rome'" (Acts 23:11).
- "And now I urge you to take heart, for there will be no loss of life among you, but only of the ship. For there stood by me this night an angel of the God to whom I belong and whom I serve, saying, do not be afraid, Paul; you must be brought before

Caesar; and indeed God has granted you all those who sail with you. Therefore take heart, men, for I believe God that it will be just as it was told me" (Acts 27:22–25).

- "It is doubtless not profitable for me to boast. I will come to visions and revelations of the Lord: I know a man in Christ who fourteen years ago—whether in the body I do not know, or whether out of the body I do not know, God knows—such a one was caught up to the third heaven. And I know such a man—whether in the body or out of the body I do not know, God knows—how he was caught up into Paradise and heard inexpressible words, which it is not lawful for a man to utter. Of such a one I will boast; yet of myself I will not boast, except in my infirmities. For though I might desire to boast, I will not be a fool; for I will speak the truth. But I refrain, lest anyone should think of me above what he sees me to be or hears from me" (2 Corinthians 12:1–6).

The apostle Paul had an abundance of revelations through the Holy Spirit, yet he humbled himself before God, because he knew it was only by the grace of God. The shipwreck incident in Acts 27 reveals that Paul was being taken to Rome to appear before Caesar, but he was in constant communication with the throne room of God Almighty. He received much assurance that God was in control of whatever circumstance he was facing at the time. The ship that Paul and other passengers boarded to Rome faced a serious storm at sea, but God through his angel assured Paul and the people with him of their safety.

Paul would not have received these revelations if he was not connected to the Spirit of God and if he was overtaken by worry. We are living at a time when many believers have become desensitized and cannot receive from the Holy Spirit because they do not pay adequate attention to the Spirit of God in them. "The spirit of a man is the lamp of the Lord, searching all the inner depths of his heart" (Proverbs 20:27). It means that your spirit cooperates with the Holy Spirit to guide and illuminate your understanding. God will guide and instruct you by your spirit, not by your emotions or feelings. We put ourselves in danger when we are not sensitive to the Holy Spirit, when we are led by our emotions or human reasoning.

It is not bad to analyze issues and display reasoning leading to a logical conclusion, but you cannot work that way with the Holy Spirit because he may tell you to do something that does not make logical sense. For example, God said to King Jehoshaphat, "Position yourselves, stand still and see the salvation of the Lord who is with you" (2 Chronicles 20:17). Although the nation of Judah faced the three enemy nations in battle at the Valley of Berachah, God gave them an overwhelming victory (2 Chronicles 20:1–32). Jehoshaphat and the people of Judah obeyed God even when it did not make sense, and ultimately, Israel defeated their enemies and carried away spoils. Sometimes, we can be in the midst of a storm or passing through the wilderness of life, but the Holy Spirit assures us that the outcome will be good. Our Lord Jesus was inside the boat asleep while the disciples were battling the storm (Mark 4:35–44). He knew that the outcome would be good, because he created the world and was in complete control (Colossians 1:15–19).

How sharp is your spiritual radar, or is it even alive? Radar is an object-detection system that uses radio waves to determine the range, angle, or velocity of objects. It can be used to detect aircraft, ships, spacecraft, guided missiles, motor vehicles, weather formations, and terrains. God wants all believers to sharpen their spiritual radar in order to detect things in the spirit realm, even before they take place here on earth. Sometimes, we become victims of circumstance because our spiritual radar was inactive due to sinful lifestyles or because we were pursuing shadows instead of the real thing.

One day, before we purchased our home, the house we were renting was foreclosed, and we faced eviction. We attempted to buy a property; we made an offer, which was accepted, scheduled a building inspection, and paid for the appraisal, but the bank did not approve the loan. We lost about $1,250. Later, we saw another property and followed the same procedure, but just before we paid for the appraisal, we discovered that the deal might not go through, and we lost about $550. Altogether, we lost $1,800. It was a painful experience to me in particular, and then I decided to observe three days of fasting and prayer. As I waited for the Lord in prayer, I asked God why he had allowed us to go into purchasing the two properties, since he knew the deal would not go through. The Holy Spirit spoke to me clearly by asking me a question: "Who told you to leave the apartment you occupied? You prayed for guidance from the Lord, but did you wait to receive an answer? Stay where you are until I instruct you on what to do."

Eventually, the eviction resulted in lawsuit that lasted for almost twelve months. During this period, my wife suggested that we vacate the apartment and discontinue the legal action. I told her that the Holy Spirit said we should remain in the apartment until we were told otherwise. She did not receive the message wholeheartedly, because she was concerned for the safety of our family. I assured her that God would protect us and that he would give us victory in the end. It was a stressful situation, but I had peace of mind throughout the ordeal. At last, the court decided in our favor, and we purchased the property, which is a three-family house. Recently, we took some equity from this three-family house and used it for a down payment to purchase a single-family house with three bedrooms.

It might surprise you to know that I had a frightening dream before we got the letter of eviction. In the dream, I saw myself approaching a strange house. In front of the house were different kinds of snakes. I was afraid and wanted to go back, but when I looked back, all I could see was thick darkness. I had no choice but to go forward and walk over the snakes. When I stepped on the snakes with my right foot, the biggest among them raised its head to bite me, and I used my right hand to hit it. It went flat on the ground, and I passed. I woke up immediately after this, and I was troubled in my spirit for many days. On account of this, I decided to observe three days of fasting and prayer. The Holy Spirit told me during the fasting that trials were coming but that God had already given me victory.

I have discovered the importance of drawing closer to God and of getting clearance in my spirit before I venture into a significant project or make a major decision in life. All children of God should endeavor to develop their spiritual radar and align it with the Holy Spirit. In so doing, we can operate on the same spiritual frequency. Believers must be in the Spirit in order to connect to God. We must endeavor to serve God in the Spirit: "For God is my witness, whom I serve with my spirit in the gospel of His Son, that without ceasing I make mention of you always in my prayers" (Romans 1:9). The apostle Paul did not serve God by reasoning, emotion, logic, willpower, senses, or head knowledge, but by his spirit.

Jesus said to the woman of Samaria, "But the hour is coming, and now is, when the true worshippers will worship the Father in spirit and truth; for the Father is seeking such to worship Him" (John 4:23). There is a big difference when we worship or serve God in the spirit as opposed to the flesh. Worshipping and serving God in the flesh is too mechanical and does not attract any reward, but when we serve him in the spirit, we influence other lives. Bear in mind that it is the Spirit that gives life, for the flesh profits nothing (John 6:63). Be watchful and maintain a consistent spiritual lifestyle. Jesus said, "Watch and pray, lest you enter into temptation. The Spirit indeed is willing, but the flesh is weak" (Mark 14:38).

You must be prayerful if you want to maintain a spiritual lifestyle consistent with the Word of God. The accuser of the brethren is always around (Revelation 12:10), but God would not want you to give him any foothold. "Be angry, and do not sin; do not let the sun go down on your wrath, nor give place to the devil" (Ephesians 4:26–27). The devil is a usurper and will take anything that does not belong to him (John 10:10). Can you imagine when you have given him a foothold? He will quickly grab it, and it will be difficult to regain it. Never allow your emotion, feelings, or human reasoning to control you; instead, give more room to the Holy Spirit, and he will guide you and also give you revelations that will surprise you.

When bad things happen, people often respond negatively by asking, "Where was God when that happened to me?" God is the revealer of secrets through the Holy Spirit, but when we are too occupied, insensitive to the Holy Spirit, or have no time to be in the secret place, we will not receive any revelation (1 Samuel 3:1). Visions from God were rare during the time of Eli, before Samuel came on the scene. God cannot force himself upon us. You must make time to hear from God if you want him to confide in you.

I had two dreams within a one-week interval; one was about a young man in his teens who was drowning in the river, and I jumped in and rescued him. The second was about a young lady in our church whom I saw wearing a cast on her right hand. She said it was due to serious burns from hot water. I understood these were not ordinary dreams, so I decided to fast for a day following the second dream. It was not clear what the devil wanted to do, but I mentioned the dreams before our whole congregation, and we all prayed about it. All of this took place before my wife had a fall in front of our church. Frankly, it was God's intervention that has kept her alive. The devil really meant to harm her, but God's Word said, "Do not touch My anointed ones and do My prophets no harm" (Psalm 105:15).

God wants us to be closer to him so that he can reveal things to us before they happen. This means we must be sensitive to the Holy Spirit's prompting and leadership. In other words, we must always attune our spiritual radar, because we are living in an evil world.

> Therefore, brethren, we are debtors not to the flesh, to live according to the flesh. For if you live according to the flesh you will die; but if by the Spirit you put to death the deeds of the body, you will live. For as many as are led by the Spirit of God, these are sons of God. (Romans 8:12–14)

A life in the flesh cannot please God, but a life in Spirit can. Whenever you notice that the flesh is taking the upper hand in your life, I recommend that you read Romans 6:1–23 and 8:1–39; and Galatians 5:1–26 every day for thirty days. I have tried it and I can tell you that it works. The Holy Spirit will enable you to regain your spiritual vitality and subdue the flesh (1 Corinthians 9:24–27).

What about teaching the Word of God? Preaching may be logical, organized properly, and presented systematically, but without the illumination of the Holy Spirit, there will be no conviction, and no souls will be saved. Sinners will continue to live their normal lives. The Holy Spirit is the one who convicts people of sin, teaches the truth about Christ, and brings all things to our remembrance (John 16:7-11). It is the Spirit who gives the Word of knowledge and bestows the spiritual gifts so we can faithfully serve the body of Christ.

"The spirit of a man will sustain him in sickness, but who can bear a broken spirit?" (Proverbs 18:14). During a time of sickness or trial, our spirit keeps us connected to the Holy Spirit to supply the strength, faith, and healing needed to recover from the infirmity. Having a broken spirit during a time of illness will drain what little energy we have left. Your spirit must be alive and active, believing and trusting that God is able to bring healing to your body just as he promised in his Word (Exodus 15:26; Psalm 107:20; Isaiah 53:1–6; Jeremiah 17:14).

I was in my office one weekend, preparing for the forthcoming Sunday service, when the Holy Spirit prompted me to take the anointing oil from the altar and go around our church building. I resisted the urge, but this inner voice persisted, and, after the third time, I suspended what I was doing, went straight to the altar, and took the anointing oil. First, I anointed the main entrance to the church and made some declarations against the works of darkness. I went around the building several times without talking to anyone, pouring anointing oil on the ground at intervals until the Holy Spirit told me it was enough. Then I went back to the church building and prayed fervently before resuming my preparations. I could not understand what the devil wanted to do; however, I knew in my spirit that the evil plans of the enemy had been aborted and rendered null and void.

I remember vividly two incidents that occurred at different times when I was alone in the church. The first happened on a Thursday afternoon as I was offloading some food items from my van. I entered the church building without knowing that someone was following behind me. After putting down the box in my hand, I turned around and was surprised to see a young man standing directly at my back. He wore a backpack and had some magazines in his hand.

He held out a magazine and said to me, "Take this; you dropped it."

I looked at the magazine, which was written in Arabic, and I said,

"No. That isn't mine." I stared at this young man, who looked Middle Eastern.

He said to me again, "Take it; it is yours."

I replied, "It is not mine." I forcefully ordered him to leave the building, but he resisted. Then, I pulled my cell phone out of my pocket to call the police. Almost immediately, he exited the building without hesitation. I finished what I was doing and then left the church premises.

The second incident happened on a Tuesday evening after our weekly Bible study. At this time, I was alone in the church, trying to put some last things away before locking the door. Suddenly, a young man entered the church building and came over to me.

He asked, "Where is the priest? I need some prayers; I need some prayers."

I said to him, "This is not the time for prayers. The Bible study ended fifteen minutes ago. Come on Sunday or next week on Tuesday."

He said, "I need prayer now."

Without hesitation, I commanded him to leave the building or I would call the police. Immediately, he exited the building, and I quickly turned off the lights, locked the doors, and left.

We are living in evil days, and we need to be sensitive to the leading of the Holy Spirit. We must not take anything for granted, especially when the Spirit of God is prompting us to do something. I cannot fathom what the devil had planned, but one thing was certain: the Lord defeated the counsel of Ahithophel (2 Samuel 15:31).

All believers must develop sensitivity to the leading of the Holy Spirit in their lives. This means learning to yield totally to him in all aspects of your life. Involve God in all your plans, and he will direct your path (Proverbs 16:3, 3:5–6). Do not do anything without the leading of the Holy Spirit. Be like Moses, who demanded the presence of God before the Israelites continued their journey in the wilderness (Exodus 33:12–17).

I will now turn to chapter five to discuss the importance of water baptism by believers.

CHAPTER 5

The Importance of Water Baptism in the Christian Faith

> Now as they went down the road, they came to some water. And the eunuch said, "See, here is water. What hinders me from being baptized?"
>
> —Acts 8:36

Jesus's instruction was, "Go therefore and make disciples of all nations, baptizing them in the name of the Father and of the Son and of the Holy Spirit" (Matthew 28:19). "And he said to them, 'Go into all the world and preach the gospel to every creature. He who believes and is baptized will be saved; but he who does not believe will be condemned'" (Mark 16:15–16).

Water baptism is important after repentance or when a person acknowledges Jesus as Lord and Savior. Baptism does not grant salvation; nevertheless, it is important that new believers go through it if they have the opportunity to do so.

The origin of Christian baptism is in Jesus Christ, who went to John the Baptist to be baptized in order to fulfill all righteousness (Matthew 3:15). The difference between Jesus's baptism and ours is that Christ had no sin in him and, therefore, didn't need to repent to be baptized. Christians are baptized after salvation by faith (Matthew 28:19; Mark 16:16). Baptism follows salvation, and not the other way around. Water baptism does not bring salvation, but it ought to take place when people accept Jesus Christ as their Lord and Savior (Acts 8:36–37). It is a requirement within the Christian community for new converts. People being baptized, and believers in general, see water baptism as a symbol of identification with Christ. The apostle Paul used the imagery of burial and resurrection to describe what takes place when a person is baptized by immersion: "Therefore we were buried with Him through baptism into death, that just as Christ was raised from the dead by the glory of the Father, even so we also should walk in newness of life" (Romans 6:4). Water baptism is an outward picture representing the inward purification from the guilt of sin. This guilt of sin is cleansed not by baptism but by the blood of Christ (Galatians 1:4, 2:20; Ephesians 1:7; Colossians 1:12–14, 19–22; Titus 2:14; 1 Peter 1:18–20; Hebrews 9:15).

Paul gives us the significance of baptism in Colossians 2:12: "Buried with Him in baptism, in which you also were raised with Him through faith in the working of God, who raised Him from the dead." Water baptism means associating or identifying with the death, burial, and resurrection of Jesus Christ. It symbolizes what has already taken place on the inside of the new believer.

Water baptism is debated among many denominations, especially infant baptism. Nevertheless, the three recognized types of baptism are sprinkling, pouring, and immersion. The one most acceptable to many evangelical churches is the immersion, because it depicts vividly the death, burial, and resurrection cited in Romans 6:4 and Colossians 2:12. In Mark 1:9–10, Jesus was baptized in the River Jordan. This cannot be done by either sprinkling or pouring, but by immersion.

Should We Baptize Infants?

Most evangelical churches believe and attest that only those who have a personal relationship with Christ should be baptized. This demonstrates that the person has made a commitment to follow Christ. An infant, though born to Christian parents, cannot understand the meaning of baptism or what it takes to make a personal commitment to Christ. Believing and confession are necessary prerequisites for salvation:

That if you confess with your mouth the Lord Jesus and believe in your heart that God has raised him from the dead, you will be saved. For with the heart one believes unto righteousness, and with the mouth confession is made unto salvation. (Romans 10:9–10)

Only those who have repented from their sins and made personal commitment to Christ are eligible for water baptism, according to the Bible.

Believer's Baptism from the Anabaptist Perspective

Believer's baptism was a major issue among the Anabaptists of the sixteenth century. In fact, it was so important to their doctrine that many of their leaders paid a heavy price, being persecuted or even executed. People like Felix Manz, Balthasar Hubmaier, Pilgram Marpeck, and Menno Simons produced important documents detailing their stand on baptism.

According to the Swiss Brethren, "Baptism signifies the forgiveness of sins, an inner transformation of mind and heart, and a pledge of a life of discipleship."[67] Baptism does not save; instead, the confession of faith in Jesus as Lord and Savior is what brings the believer into a new relationship with God. The Swiss Brethren also stated, "Baptism means nothing else than a dying of the old man, and a putting on of the new."[68] The Anabaptists believed that baptism should be reserved for only committed disciples. "Baptism ought to be administered to all who have been taught repentance and a change of life and in truth believe their sins to have been blotted out through Christ ... and who wish to be buried with him into death that they may be able to rise again with him."[69] They also viewed baptism as "a symbol of initiation into the church and a sign of the new life which the believer

---

[67] William R. Estep, *The Anabaptist Story: An Introduction to Sixteenth-Century Anabaptism*, 3rd ed. (Grand Rapids, MI: Eerdmans, 1996), 202.

[68] Ibid., 203.

[69] Ibid., 205.

has in Christ … it has no meaning where faith in Christ is absent."[70] Anabaptist brethren also believed that "baptism is a public confession and testimony of an inward faith, and also a pledge of discipleship in which the candidate promises in the future to live according to the word and command of Christ."[71] They believed that "baptism by water should not be administered without previous profession of faith."[72]

Regarding believer's baptism and discipleship, the Anabaptist brethren stated,

> Now when a man confesses that he is a sinner, believes in the remission of sins, and has committed himself to a new life, he must then testify outwardly before the church of Christ … that he accepts the word of Christ in his heart, and is minded to surrender himself to live in [the] future according to the word, will and law of Christ … Then he must be baptized in water; by which means he publicly professes his faith and purpose … If he should in the future bring reproach or blame upon the name of Christ through public or grievous sins, he promises to submit to punishment by his brethren, according to the command of Christ (Matt. 18).[73]

Anabaptist brethren believed that "infant baptism was out of step with New Testament character of baptism. Furthermore, that infant baptism is a deception invented and introduced by men."[74] Infant baptism is contrary to the practices of the New Testament church. There is no example of children being baptized in the New Testament. We were commanded to baptize those who believe (Matthew 28:19–20; Mark 16:15–18). Some people have argued that when the whole household believed the gospel, repented of their sins, and were baptized,

---

[70] Ibid., 206.
[71] Ibid., 208.
[72] Ibid., 209.
[73] Ibid., 212.
[74] Ibid., 219.

for example in Acts 16:32–33, that infants and children must have been included in the baptism. The Bible is silent on this, and we should consider that as the final word.

The Anabaptists provided a summary of their belief on baptism:

> No element or outward object in this world can purify the soul; only faith can cleanse the heart of man. So, it follows that baptism is no washing away of sins. But though it cannot wash them away, yet it is of God. So, it must be a public profession of an inward faith. As to whether the children of Christians and children in Old Testament times are the children of God, we leave that to Him who alone knows all things.[75]

This debate has been on for ages, but it is important that we base our teachings and belief system on the Word of God, the Bible.

Summary

We have discussed the importance of knowing that we have eternal life once we surrender our lives to Jesus Christ. Assurance of salvation is a wonderful concept in the New Testament, and all believers must receive this reality in themselves, because the Holy Spirit in us bears witness of who we are. "The Spirit Himself bears witness with our spirit that we are children of God, and if children, then heirs—heirs of God and joint heirs with Christ, if indeed we suffer with Him, that we may also be glorified together" (Romans 8:16–17).

After this issue of knowing that we are in Christ is settled, every new believer goes through the discipleship process, which is represented by the five fingers: studying the Word of God, having an effective prayer life, engaging in effective evangelism, being in constant fellowship with members of the body of Christ, and living a life of worship and constant praise to God. Christian discipleship is paramount in the life of every

---

[75] Ibid., 218.

believer because it lays a firm foundation for a child of God to live a victorious life.

We also noted the importance of water baptism, if one has the opportunity to do so; because it is one of the ordinances that Jesus commanded us to carry out as his disciples.

Bibliography

Barton, Bruce B. *The Life Application Study Commentary.* Carol Stream, IL: Tyndale, 1997.

Coleman, Robert E. *The Master Plan of Evangelism.* Grand Rapids, MI: Baker, 1993.

Estep, William, R. *The Anabaptist Story: An Introduction to Sixteenth-Century Anabaptism.* 3ʳᵈ ed. Grand Rapids, MI: Eerdmans, 1996.

Fellowship Tract League, Lebanon, Ohio.

Grady, J. Lee. "Six Principles of Christian Discipleship" presentation at International Fellowship of Christian Assemblies Convention, August 5–7, 2017, Sandusky, Ohio.

Jeremiah, David. *The Jeremiah Study Bible Commentary.* Nashville, TN: Worthy, 2013.

Jones, Jeffrey D. *Traveling Together: A Guide for Disciple-Forming Congregations.* Lanham, MD: Rowman & Littlefield, 2006.

Kennedy, D. James. *Evangelism Explosion: Equipping Churches for Friendship, Evangelism, Discipleship, and Healthy Growth.* 4ᵗʰ ed. Carol Stream, IL: Tyndale, 1996.

Myers, Allen C. *The Eerdmans Bible Dictionary.* Grand Rapids, MI: Eerdmans, 1987.

Umejiaku, Chima E. *Pursuit of Spiritual Renewal: A Call to Corporate and Individual Revival*. Maitland, FL: Xulon Press, 2017.

Watson, David. *Called & Committed: World-Changing Discipleship*. Wheaton, IL: Harold Shaw, 1989.

Watson, David Lowes. *Covenant Discipleship: Christian Formation through Mutual Accountability*. Nashville, TN: Discipleship Resource Publications, 1989.

Walvoord, John F., and Roy B. Zuck, eds. *The Bible Knowledge Commentary: An Exposition of the Scriptures by Dallas Seminary Faculty*. Vol. 2, *New Testament*. Colorado Springs, CO: Chariot Victor, 1983.

White, James F. *A Brief History of Christian Worship*. Nashville, TN: Abingdon, 1993.

White, James F. *Introduction to Christian Worship*. 3rd ed. Nashville, TN: Abingdon, 2000.

Youngblood, Ronald F., ed. F. F. Bruce and R. K. Harrison, contributing eds. *Nelson's New Illustrated Bible Dictionary*. Rev. ed. Nashville, TN: Thomas Nelson, 1995.

Notes

1   Discipleship Tools: The Discipleship Resources and Tools you need to have to grow in yourfaith: "What Is Christian character?". Accessed July 25, 2019, https. www.discipleshiptools.org

2   Merriam-Webster's Collegiate Dictionary. 10th ed. Springfield, MA: Webster's, 1998.

Printed in the United States
By Bookmasters